Solutions Manual

To accompany *Meaningful Statistics*

by

Matt Davis

THIRD CUSTOM EDITION

Custom Publishing

New York   Boston   San Francisco
London   Toronto   Sydney   Tokyo   Singapore   Madrid
Mexico City   Munich   Paris   Cape Town   Hong Kong   Montreal

Cover Art: Courtesy of DigitalVision/Getty Images.

Printed in the United States of America

10 9 8 7 6 5 4 3 2 1

2009360412

JK

Pearson
Custom Publishing
is a division of

www.pearsonhighered.com

ISBN 10: 0-558-31506-2
ISBN 13: 978-0-558-31506-1

Table of Contents

Chapter 1

Chapter 2

Chapter 3

Chapter 4

Chapter 5

Chapter 6

Chapter 7

Chapter 8

Chapter 9

Chapter 10

Chapter 11

Section 1.1:

1) When you are only seeking to organize or summarize your data, this is referred to as <u>descriptive</u> statistics.

2) When you attempt to draw conclusions about the population, based on information you obtained from a sample, that is known as <u>inferential</u> statistics.

3) The group of people or things you wish to state your conclusions about is known as the <u>population</u>.

4) The <u>sample</u> is the part of the population that your data is collected from.

5) a) the population
   b) descriptive

7) a) a sample
   b) inferential

9) a) the population
   b) descriptive

Section 1.2:

11) An Observational study is one where the researchers simply collect <u>natural</u> data. This type <u>can not</u> show cause and effect.

12) A designed experiment is one where the researchers design and <u>controls</u> the experiment. This type <u>can</u> show cause and effect.

13) a) Observational. This is a life-long study and to be designed, the researcher would have to control the amount of sleep for the participants for their entire lives.
    b) No, because we can't prove cause and effect in an observational study.

14) a) Designed. The researchers are controlling the choice of the participants whether or not to take the medication or a placebo.
    b) Yes, the results of a designed study can show cause and effect.

15) a) Designed. The farmer decided whether or not each plant received the fertilizer.
    b) Yes, since it is a designed study.

17) a) Designed. The teach randomly split the students into the two groups and required one group to do the homework.
    b) Yes, since it is a designed study.

Section 1.3:

19) When you collect data from the entire population of interest, that is known as taking a <u>census</u>. Two disadvantages of this are that it can be <u>destructive</u> or <u>expensive</u>.

20) To minimize our sampling error, we want our samples to be <u>representative</u> rather than biased. This means that the sample contains all the relevant characteristics of the population in the same <u>proportion</u> as they exist in the population.

21) The procedure were each possible sample of a given size is equally likely to be the one chosen is referred to as <u>simple</u> <u>random</u> <u>sample</u>.

22) a) Cluster Sampling
    b) Stratified Sampling
    c) Systematic Sampling

23) On the calculator, choose MATH > PRB > RANDINT(1,20) and then press ENTER 10 times. Repeats are allowed. Answers will vary due to random selection.

25) On the calculator, choose MATH > PRB > RANDINT(20,60) and then press ENTER repeatedly. Ignore repeats. Write down results until you have 15 different values. Answers will vary due to random selection.

27) STEP 1: N = 100, n = 12 $\Rightarrow \dfrac{100}{12} \approx 8.33 \Rightarrow k = 8$
    STEP 2: On the calculator, choose MATH > PRB > randInt(1,8). The result is m.
    STEP 3: Sample is:
    $m, m + k, m + 2k, \ldots, m + 11k$
    Answers will vary due to random selection.

29) Let the tables be the clusters. The tables are probably numbered from 1 to 50, so choose 6 numbers without replacement using randInt(1, 50). Then select all the players at the selected table numbers.

31) Dems: $0.517 * 980 = 506.66$
    Reps: $0.431 * 980 = 422.38$
    Other: $0.052 * 980 = 50.96$
    Rounding to the nearest who number, we get 507 Dems, 422 Reps, and 51 Others.

33) Choosing all the students from one location on campus will not give all math students an equal chance at being chosen. Students in the math lab are motivated and tend to study more. This sample will probably skew the result towards a higher than actual mean study time.

35) When people choose on their own whether or not to participate in the study, it is never the case that all people will be equally likely to be a part of the sample. In addition, in such polls, people are allowed to vote repeatedly. How this will effect the results is not clear, but in the past, web sites have encouraged large groups of people to vote favorably for the worst singer.

37) If you wait until you see data that supports something you wish to prove, your chance of "proving" it increases. If this player has played in over 1000 tournaments and is an average player, then this should happen somewhere in his results.

Section 1.4:

39) A variable that takes on non-numeric values is known as a <u>categorical</u> variable.

40) If the variable takes on numeric values, then in is known as a <u>quantitative</u> variable.

41) Quantitative variables whose possible values have <u>gaps</u> between them are known as discrete.

42) Quantitative variables whose possible values do not have gaps between them, but rather form an <u>interval</u> are known as continuous.

43) a) The selected student's favorite beverage
    b) Sarsaparilla
    c) Categorical

45) a) The selected Californian's number of speeding tickets in the last 3 years.
    b) Zero
    c) Quantitative – Discrete

47) a) The height of the selected Giraffe.
    b) 17.3 feet tall
    c) Quantitative – Continuous

49) a) The type of food chosen.
    b) Pizza.
    c) Categorical

51) a) The breaking distance for the selected SUV
    b) 87.4 feet
    c) Quantitative – Continuous

Chapter Problem:

a) Since the percentages for each group are not given, we must calculate them using fractions. In the population the percentage of households earning less than $25K is given by $\frac{387}{1973} \approx 0.1961 = 19.61\%$. To determine the number of such households, we take this percentage times the sample size. So we get: $\frac{387}{1973} * 50 \approx 9.81$. Similarly for $25K – < $50K we get $\frac{562}{1973} * 50 \approx 14.24$. Rounding these to the nearest integer, we get 10 from less than $25K, 14 from $25K – < $50K.

b) Percentage of gross household income given to charity.

c) 9.3%

d) Quantitative – Continuous

Section 2.1:

1) The left hand boundary of the class description is called the lower <u>cutpoint</u> and the right hand boundary is called the <u>upper</u> <u>cutpoint</u>.

2) The number of items in each class is known as the <u>frequency</u> of the class.

3) The ratio of the number of items in each class to the total number of items in the data set is known as the <u>relative</u> <u>frequency</u>.

4) The midpoint of a class is the <u>average</u> of the lower and upper cutpoints. This value is often used as a representative for the data values in that class when making computations.

5) The difference between consecutive lower cutpoints is known as the class <u>width</u>.

6) We use the - < symbols when grouping <u>continuous</u> data, but we just use the – symbol alone when grouping <u>discrete</u> data.

7)

Points	Frequency	Rel Freq	Midpoints
0 – 4	1	0.0159	2
5 – 9	5	0.0794	7
10 – 14	6	0.0952	12
15 – 19	19	0.3016	17
20 – 24	16	0.2540	22
25 – 29	9	0.1429	27
30 – 34	4	0.0635	32
35 - 39	3	0.0476	37
	63	1.0001	

9)

Nickname	Frequency	Rel Freq
49ers	5	0.1220
Steelers	5	0.1220
Cowboys	5	0.1220
Packers	3	0.0732
Raiders	3	0.0732
Redskins	3	0.0732
Patriots	3	0.0732
Colts	2	0.0488
Dolphins	2	0.0488
Giants	2	0.0488
Broncos	2	0.0488
Jets	1	0.0244
Chiefs	1	0.0244
Bears	1	0.0244
Rams	1	0.0244
Ravens	1	0.0244
Buccaneers	1	0.0244
	41	1.0004

11)
a)

Time	Freq	Rel Freq	Midpoints
3.5 - < 4.0	1	0.0222	3.75
4.0 - < 4.5	7	0.1556	4.25
4.5 - < 5.0	8	0.1778	4.75
5.0 - < 5.5	7	0.1556	5.25
5.5 - < 6.0	4	0.0889	5.75
6.0 - < 6.5	9	0.2000	6.25
6.5 - < 7.0	5	0.1111	6.75
7.0 - < 7.5	3	0.0667	7.25
7.5 - < 8.0	1	0.0222	7.75
	45	1.0001	

b) Not really only 4 out of 45 or 8.89% lasted that long.

13)
a)

Score	Freq	Rel Freq	Midpoints
20 – 29	2	0.0526	24.5
30 – 39	1	0.0263	34.5
40 – 49	5	0.1316	44.5
50 – 59	2	0.0526	54.5
60 – 69	6	0.1579	64.5
70 – 79	8	0.2105	74.5
80 – 89	7	0.1842	84.5
90 – 99	6	0.1579	94.5
100 – 109	1	0.0263	104.5
	38	0.9999	

b) 8 + 7 + 6 + 1 scored 70 or higher. That is 22 out of 38 or about 57.89%.

15) a)

Score	Frequency	Rel Freq
0	2	0.0465
1	0	0.0000
2	3	0.0698
3	6	0.1395
4	22	0.5116
5	10	0.2326
	43	1.0000

b) All but 5 of the students met the teacher's expectations (or hope). That means that 38 out of 43 or about 88.37% met the expectation. This meets the description of "most of the students", so the teacher is probably satisfied with that.

Section 2.2:

17) For a standard histogram, the bars are drawn from <u>lower cutpoint</u> to <u>lower cutpoint</u>. So, unless there is an empty class, there will be no <u>gaps</u> between the bars.

18) When doing a histogram for single value grouping, the bars start and end at <u>half</u> marks.

19) For categorical data, there is no natural flow from one bar to the next, so we do put <u>gaps</u> between the bars.

20) For histograms, we label the <u>number</u> line, but for bar charts we label the <u>bars</u>.

21) For dotplots, if data values are repeated or if they are very close to each other, then we <u>stack</u> the dots.

22) If an inconsistent scale chops off the bottom of all our bars, this throws off the proportions between the bars. Such graphs can be <u>misleading</u>.

23) a)

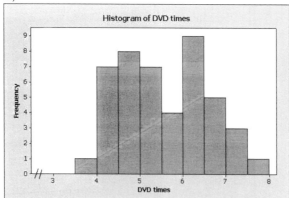

Notes: The bars go from lower cutpoint to lower cutpoint. No gaps exist between the bars. The double slash mark on the horizontal axis indicates a break in scale.

b)

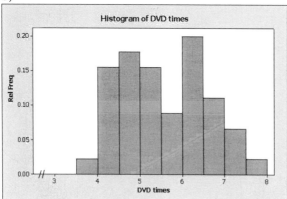

c) Despite the difference in vertical scale, they both give the same visual impression.

25)

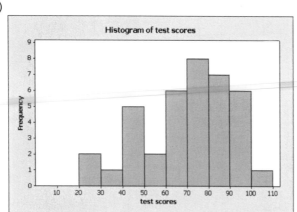

Notes: Even though the data is discrete and the first class is 20 – 29, the bars still go from lower cutpoint to lower cutpoint, so the first bar goes from 20 to 30 (no gaps.) Zero is in its standard location, so we do not need to draw in the double slash mark.

27)

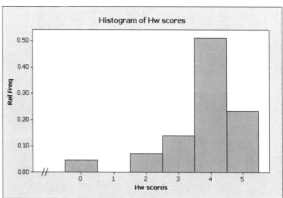

Notes: Because this is single value grouping, the bars are centered around the value of the class. For whole numbers like this, that means the bars go from 1/2 mark to 1/2 mark. The first bar goes from –0.5 to 0.5. The last bar goes from 4.5 to 5.5.

29) a)

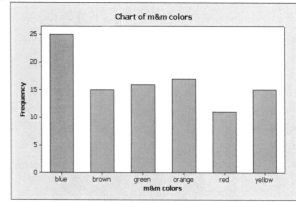

Notes: For categorical data, there is no numbering on the horizontal axis. We just write the description under each bar. Also, for categorical data we put gaps between the bars.

b)

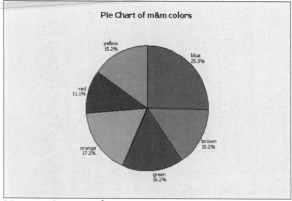

Notes: Start with easy percentages like 25.25% that make up about 1/4 of the graph. Then look for nice sums. For example Yellow plus Red makes up about 25%.

31) a)

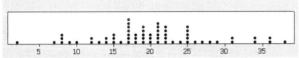

Notes: There is no vertical axis for dotplots. Remember to stack values that are the same or very similar.

b) Most games he scored between 12 and 25 pts. Scores above 31 or below 7 were rare.

33) a) Since the bar appears to be 4 or 5 times as tall, it appears that that class has 4 or 5 times the data in it.

b) The bottom of the bars is drawn from a height of 155 rather than from the proper height of 0. This mistake greatly exaggerates the differences in heights.

Section 2.3:

35) Because a stem-and-leaf diagram is looked at like a histogram, it is extremely important that we have consistent <u>spacing</u> between the numbers.

36) For a standard stem-and-leaf diagram, the width of the classes is <u>10</u>. If we use two lines per stem, then the width is <u>5</u>.

37) a) **Note**: It is very helpful to use the calculator to sort the data for you before you get started. Do this by choosing STAT > EDIT and the entering the data set in L1. After data is entered press STAT > SORTA(L1) > ENTER.

```
0 |278889
1 |022344555677777788899999
2 |000111112222234555556789
3 |1144668
```

b)
```
0 |2
0 |78889
1 |022344
1 |5556777777788899999
2 |0001111112222234
2 |555556789
3 |1144
3 |668
```
Note: switching to 2 lines per stem changes the classes from 0 – 9, 10 – 19, etc., to 0 – 4, 5 – 9, 10 – 14, 15 – 19, etc.

c) I think that two lines per stem was better. The first one didn't have enough classes to show the scoring patterns.

39) a) **Note**: See sorting tip on solution to (37).
```
 2 |29
 3 |7
 4 |15679
 5 |04
 6 |112268
 7 |23456699
 8 |0013669
 9 |013469
10 |8
```

b) Most of the scores are above 60. Failing scores (below 50) were more rare.

41) Leaf Unit is the 10s place
```
 0 |9
 1 |358
 2 |00235555
 3 |000003555
 4 |00
 5 |
 6 |05
 8 |
 9 |0
10 |
11 |0
12 |
13 |
14 |
15 |0
16 |
17 |
18 |
19 |
20 |
21 |
22 |
23 |
24 |
25 |
26 |
27 |
28 |
29 |
30 |
31 |
32 |
33 |
34 |
35 |
36 |
37 |
38 |0
```
Notes: The empty classes are shown on the diagram. This helps us see how unusual the 3800 value is. Since we are using the 10s digit for the leaves, we use the 100s digit for the stem. 2 digit stems are allowed, but 2 digit leaves are not. When the leaf unit is not the ones place, a note should be added stated the value of the leaf unit.

Section 2.4:

43) If the left and right hand sides of a distribution are mirror images of one another, then we refer to that as a <u>symmetric</u> distribution.

44) If a graph has extreme values on one side, but not on the other, then it is referred to as either a left or right <u>skewed</u> distribution.

45) When we look at the graph of sample data, we are not actually trying to determine the shape of the sample, rather we are trying to determine the shape of the distribution of the <u>population</u> from which it was taken.

46) It can be difficult to determine the distribution of the population from sample data if the sample size is too <u>small</u> .

47) a) None of those. It shows some characteristics of a right skewed distribution, but there is not enough data to make the smooth shape that is required.
    b) Right skewed. Most of the data in the sample is on the left side and the extremes are on the right.
    c) If the sample size was bigger. More sample data gives us a better view of the true population shape.

49) Right skewed. The tallest bars are on the left side and the shorter ones are on the right. The tail on the right isn't that long, so this is not really severely skewed.

51) a) Since sample looks roughly right-skewed, the best choice for the distribution of the population would be right-skewed.
    b) If the sample size was larger.

53) This time I would choose left-skewed. Most of the data is stacked up on the right with the extremes forming a tail on the left.

55) a) The sample looks like none of those, but for the population, it could be uniform. I say this because there are high and low spots all the way across the graph. This could be from a uniform population with the variation just due to the random sampling process.
    b) Perhaps if the sample size was quite larger, the effect of the randomness would be diminished and we would see a flat uniform type graph emerge.

Chapter Problem:

a)

Receipts	Frequency	Rel Freq	Midpoints
250 - < 300	3	0.12	275
300 - < 350	9	0.36	325
350 - < 400	5	0.20	375
400 - < 450	6	0.24	425
450 - < 500	1	0.04	475
500 - < 550	0	0.00	525
550 - < 600	0	0.00	575
600 - < 650	1	0.04	625
	25	1.00	

b)

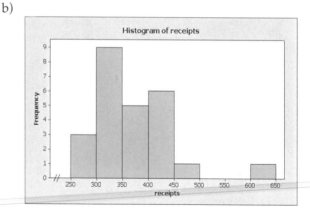

c) It's hard to say for sure because no obvious shape is emerging. It might be right-skewed because the tallest bar is on the left and it has extreme values only on the right.

d) No. This is not a random sample of movies. It is a top 25 list. The histogram of a random sample gives us a hint at the shape of the population, but this is not a random sample.

Section 3.1:

1) The median of an odd data set is the value in the <u>middle</u> of the ordered list. If the number of values is even, then the median is the <u>mean</u> of the two middle values.

2) L_M stands for the <u>location</u> of the median.

3) The mean is the <u>balancing</u> point of a data set. The value of the mean is affected by <u>extremes</u> in the data set.

4) The mode is the data value that is <u>repeated</u> the most. If no values are repeated, then we say that there is <u>no mode</u>.

5) Mean: It sounds like we have all the games played, so this is population data. So we get:

$$\mu = \frac{\sum x}{N} = \frac{24}{15} = 1.6$$

Median: Start by putting the data in order: {0, 0, 0, 1, 1, 1, 1, 1, 2, 2, 2, 2, 3, 4, 4}. Now use the location formula.

$$L_M = \frac{1}{2}(15+1) = 8 \Rightarrow M = 1$$

$$L_M = \frac{1}{2}(N+1) = 8 \Rightarrow M = 1$$

Mode: The mode is the most repeated value, so the mode is 1.

7) Mean: The data for the entire year is given, so this is population data.

$$\mu = \frac{\sum x}{N} = \frac{2318}{12} \approx 193.17$$

Median: Start by ordering the data set. {104, 117, 134, 152, 172, 172, 206, 214, 236, 263, 274}

$$L_M = \frac{1}{2}(12+1) = 6.5 \Rightarrow M = \frac{172+206}{2} = 189$$

Mode: There is a two-way tie for the most repeated value, thus we have 2 modes.
Modes: 172, 274

9) The prices for ALL the resorts are given, so we have population data.

a) $\mu = \dfrac{\sum x}{N} = \dfrac{93}{16} = 58.1875$
(or $\mu \approx \$58.19$)

b) Start by sorting the data set: {30, 35, 38, 47, 48, 52, 58, 59, 62, 63, 68, 70, 72, 74, 77, 78}

$$L_M = \frac{1}{2}(16+1) = 8.5 \Rightarrow M = \frac{59+62}{2} = 60.5$$

c) Since the mean is below the median, this data set is at least a bit left skewed.

11) All the puppies in the litter are listed, so we have population data. Remember to sort the data for the median.

a) Mean: $\mu = \dfrac{\sum x}{N} = \dfrac{111.6}{9} = 12.4$

Median: $L_M = \dfrac{1}{2}(9+1) = 5 \Rightarrow M = 12.6$

b) 6 of the 9 weights are above average, so, we get $\frac{6}{9} \approx 66.67\%$.

c) Intuitively, people often expect 1/2 of the data to be below average and 1/2 of the data set to be above average. However, this does not need to be the case. Almost any % can make sense. So, YES!

13) Data for all of the homes on the street is given, so this is population data.

a) Mean:

$$\mu = \frac{\sum x}{N} = \frac{4597}{9} \approx 510.778 \Rightarrow \$510,778$$

Median: (of sorted data)

$$L_M = \frac{1}{2}(9+1) = 5 \Rightarrow M = 517 \Rightarrow \$517,000$$

b) Mean:

$$\mu = \frac{\sum x}{N} = \frac{4997}{9} \approx 555.222 \Rightarrow \$555,222$$

Median: (of sorted data)

$$L_M = \frac{1}{2}(9+1) = 5 \Rightarrow M = 517 \Rightarrow \$517,000$$

c) The mean is affected by extreme values, but the median is not. We say that the median is resistant to extremes.

15) a) Mode. Mode is the only one that works for categorical data. Its job is to find the most common value.

    b) The mean. Average income makes sense since all this money is earned by the same person. The result might be helpful in planning a budget.

    c) Median. People who hear this result will probably use it to decide whether they are in the top or bottom half of wage earners. If they used the mean, it would be skewed to the right of the middle by people with extremely high incomes.

Section 3.2:

17) The range of a data set can be found by subtracting the <u>minimum</u> from the <u>maximum</u>.

18) The standard deviation measures the amount of <u>dispersion</u> in a data set.

19) The more dispersion a data set has, the <u>larger</u> its standard deviation will be.

20) When rounding a standard deviation, use at least <u>5 digits</u> in your answer.

21) a) $R = \text{max} - \text{min} = 20 - 3 = 17$

    b) This is stated to be population data.

x	$x - \mu$	$(x - \mu)^2$
3	-9.43	88.9249
13	0.57	0.3249
11	-1.43	2.0449
10	-2.43	5.9049
20	7.57	57.3049
18	5.57	31.0249
12	-0.43	0.1849
87	-0.01	185.7143

$$\mu = \frac{\sum x}{N} = \frac{87}{7} \approx 12.43$$

$$\sigma = \sqrt{\frac{\sum (x - \mu)^2}{N}} = \sqrt{\frac{185.7143}{7}} \approx 5.1508$$

23) Data set I: $\mu_1 = \dfrac{\sum x}{N} = \dfrac{133}{5} = 26.6$ and

$$\sigma_1 = \sqrt{\frac{\sum (x - \mu_1)^2}{N}} = \sqrt{\frac{981.2}{5}} \approx 14.009$$

Data set II: $\mu_2 = \dfrac{\sum x}{N} = \dfrac{283}{5} = 56.6$ and

$$\sigma_2 = \sqrt{\frac{\sum (x - \mu_2)^2}{N}} = \sqrt{\frac{237.2}{5}} \approx 6.8877$$

So, since data set one has the larger standard deviation, it is the set with more overall dispersion. The larger the standard deviation, the more overall dispersion a data set has.

25) a) $R = \text{max} - \text{min} = 274 - 104 = 170$
We have the entire year's bills, so this is population data.

x	$x - \mu$	$(x - \mu)^2$
274	80.83	6533.49
236	42.83 *	1834.41
172	-21.17 *	448.17
152	-41.17 *	1694.97
104	-89.17	7951.29
117	-76.17	5801.87
134	-59.17	3501.09
172	-21.17 *	448.17
214	20.83 *	433.89
206	12.83 *	164.61
274	80.83	6533.49
263	69.83	4876.23
2318	-0.04	40221.67

$$\mu = \frac{2318}{12} \approx 193.17 \text{ and}$$

$$\sigma = \sqrt{\frac{\sum (x - \mu)^2}{N}} = \sqrt{\frac{40221.67}{12}} \approx 57.895$$

    b) 6 out of the 12 deviations are smaller than 57.895 (marked with a * in the middle column of the table above.) So we get:

$$\frac{6}{12} = 50\% \text{ of the data values lie within 1}$$

standard deviation of the mean.

27) a) All 9 of the puppies are represented. This is population data.

x	$x - \mu$	$(x-\mu)^2$
12.9	0.5 *	0.25
14.3	1.9	3.61
11.7	-0.7 *	0.49
13.4	1.0 *	1.00
10.2	-2.2	4.84
12.5	0.1 *	0.01
12.6	0.2 *	0.04
13.6	1.2 *	1.44
10.4	-2.0	4.00
111.6	0.0	15.68

$$\mu = \frac{111.6}{9} = 12.4 \text{ and}$$

$$\sigma = \sqrt{\frac{\sum(x-\mu)^2}{N}} = \sqrt{\frac{15.68}{9}} \approx 1.3199$$

b) $\frac{6}{9} \approx 66.67\%$ (See the values marked in the middle column of the table above.)

29) a) We have all the homes on the street, so this is population data.

x	$x - \mu$	$(x-\mu)^2$
525	14.22 *	202.2084
523	12.22 *	149.3284
517	6.22 *	38.6884
461	-49.78	2478.0484
598	87.22	7607.3284
559	48.22	2325.1684
477	-33.78 *	1141.0884
430	-80.78	6525.4084
507	-3.78 *	14.2884
4597	-0.02	20481.5556

$$\mu = \frac{4597}{9} \approx 510.78 \text{ and}$$

$$\sigma = \sqrt{\frac{\sum(x-\mu)^2}{N}} = \sqrt{\frac{20481.5556}{9}} \approx 47.705$$

b) $\frac{5}{9} \approx 55.56\%$ (see the values marked with a * in the table above.)

c) For this one we look at how many of the deviations, $x - \mu$, are smaller than $2\sigma = 95.41$. Looking at the middle column of the table, we see that they all are, so $\frac{9}{9} = 100\%$.

31) a) The problem states that we have the prices for all of the resorts, so this is population data.

x	$x - \mu$	$(x-\mu)^2$
63	4.8 *	23.04
78	19.8	392.04
30	-28.2	795.24
59	0.8 *	0.64
58	-0.2 *	0.04
77	18.8	353.44
47	-11.2 *	125.44
72	13.8 *	190.44
70	11.8 *	139.24
48	-10.2 *	104.04
62	3.8 *	14.44
35	-23.2	538.24
52	-6.2 *	38.44
74	15.8	249.64
38	-20.2	408.04
68	9.8 *	96.04
931	-0.2	3468.44

$$\mu = \frac{931}{16} = 58.1875 \approx 58.2 \text{ and}$$

$$\sigma = \sqrt{\frac{\sum(x-\mu)^2}{N}} = \sqrt{\frac{3468.44}{16}} \approx 14.723$$

Note: Even though we had an exact value available for the mean, it is much easier to use the rounded version when making the table.

b) $\frac{10}{16} = 62.5\%$ (See the values marked with an * in the chart above.)

c) $2\sigma = 29.446 \Rightarrow \frac{16}{16} = 100\%$

Section 3.3:

33) $\bar{x}$ is the symbol for the <u>sample</u> mean and μ is the symbol for the <u>population</u> mean.

34) σ is the symbol for the <u>population</u> standard deviation and s is the symbol for the <u>sample</u> standard deviation.

35) When calculating the mean and standard deviation for data that has been grouped into classes, use the <u>midpoint</u> of each class in place of the x-values.

36) In problems asking you to compute the mean and standard deviation of a data set, the value of $\sum x^2$ is given as a <u>check</u> of your data entry.

37) The problem states that this is sample data.
Median: This data is already sorted and we do
sample medians the exact same way as a
population median.

$$L_M = \frac{1}{2}(6+1) = 3.5 \Rightarrow M = \frac{8.5+9}{2} = 8.75$$

Mean and Standard Deviation:

x	$(x-\bar{x})^2$
7.5	1.172889
8	0.339889
8.5	0.006889
9	0.173889
9	0.173889
9.5	0.840889
51.5	2.708334

$$\bar{x} = \frac{\sum x}{n} = \frac{51.5}{6} \approx 8.583 \text{ and}$$

$$s = \sqrt{\frac{\sum (x-\bar{x})^2}{n-1}} = \sqrt{\frac{2.708334}{5}} \approx 0.73598$$

39) The problem states that this is sample data.

x	f	xf	$(x-\bar{x})^2 f$
0	11	0	94.4339
1	6	6	22.3494
2	7	14	6.0543
3	13	39	0.0637
4	19	76	21.7531
5	14	70	59.9886
	70	205	204.643

$$\bar{x} = \frac{\sum xf}{n} = \frac{205}{70} \approx 2.93 \text{ and}$$

$$s = \sqrt{\frac{\sum (x-\bar{x})^2 f}{n-1}} = \sqrt{\frac{204.643}{69}} \approx 1.7222$$

41) We are only looking to summarize the year and
we have all of the data for the year, so this is
population data.
a) Enter the data into L1 and then choose
STAT > CALC > 1-Var Stats L1. Remember
to verify data entry by checking the value
of $\sum x^2$. $\mu = 192.25$ and $\sigma \approx 58.308$

b) We begin by calculating the values that are
exactly 1 standard deviation on each side
of the mean. We then count the number of
data values that lie within these
boundaries.

$$\begin{matrix} \mu - \sigma = 133.942 \\ \mu + \sigma = 250.558 \end{matrix} \Rightarrow \frac{7}{12} \approx 58.33\%$$

43) The problem states that this is sample data.
a) Enter the data set into L1. Choose STAT >
CALC > 1 Var Stats L1.
$\bar{x} = 1.55 \quad s \approx 0.10453$
b) Calculate the values that are exactly 1
standard deviation on each side of the
mean and then count the number of data
values that lie within these boundaries.

$$\begin{matrix} \mu - \sigma = 1.44547 \\ \mu + \sigma = 1.65453 \end{matrix} \Rightarrow \frac{24}{36} \approx 66.67\%$$

45) We are just summarizing the scores for the
golfers we have, so they are the population
of interest in this problem.
a) Enter the data set into L1. Choose STAT >
CALC > 1 Var Stats L1.
$\mu \approx 92.65 \quad \sigma \approx 7.4810$
Note: we must write the zero at the end of
the standard deviation, because we are
required to have at least 5 digits in our
answer.

b) $$\begin{matrix} \mu - \sigma = 85.169 \\ \mu + \sigma = 100.131 \end{matrix} \Rightarrow \frac{17}{23} \approx 73.91\%$$

c) This time we must calculate the values
that lie exactly 2 standard deviations
away from the mean.

$$\begin{matrix} \mu - 2\sigma = 77.688 \\ \mu + 2\sigma = 107.612 \end{matrix} \Rightarrow \frac{22}{23} \approx 95.65\%$$

47) The problem states that this is sample data.
a) STAT > CALC > 1 Var Stats L1 yields
$\bar{x} \approx 1.48 \quad s \approx 2.4396$

b) $$\begin{matrix} \bar{x} - s = -0.9596 \\ \bar{x} + s = 3.9196 \end{matrix} \Rightarrow \frac{23}{27} \approx 85.19\%$$

Note: We only count values that lie
between the boundaries. Therefore, we
only count values from 0 to 3. We do not
round and include the 4s which are actually
more than 1 standard deviation from the
mean.

c) $$\begin{matrix} \bar{x} - 2s = -3.3992 \\ \bar{x} + 2s = 6.3592 \end{matrix} \Rightarrow \frac{26}{27} \approx 96.30\%$$

49) The problem implies that we have all of the art for this studio and that we are only seeking to summarize the data. This implies that this is population data.

a) STAT > CALC > 1 Var Stats L1 yields
$\mu \approx 480.6 \quad \sigma \approx 429.82$

b) $\begin{matrix} \mu - \sigma = 50.78 \\ \mu + \sigma = 910.42 \end{matrix} \Rightarrow \dfrac{42 - 2 - 6}{42} \approx 80.95\%$

Note: It is often easier to subtract the values outside of the boundaries away from the total.

c) $\begin{matrix} \mu - 2\sigma = 50.78 \\ \mu + 2\sigma = 910.42 \end{matrix} \Rightarrow \dfrac{40}{42} \approx 95.24\%$

51) From exercise (47) we know this is sample data.

a) Enter the number of violations in L1 and the frequencies in L2. Choose STAT > CALC > 1 Var Stats L1, L2. This gives us
$\bar{x} \approx 1.48 \quad s \approx 2.4396$
Note: This is the same data set as problem (47). It has just been grouped. Therefore, it still only contains one variable, the number of violations. Frequency is not a variable.

b) Because we are using single value grouping, we are using the actual data values to make the computations (rather than using midpoints to guess at the data values).

53) From exercise (49), we know this is pop data.

a) Determine the midpoint for each of the classes: 99.5, 299.5, . . . , 2099.5. Enter these values into L1. Enter the frequencies into L2. Choose STAT > CALC > 1 Var Stats L1, L2 and press ENTER.
$\mu \approx 489.98 , \ \sigma \approx 418.51$

b) Because we are using midpoints to guess at the actual data values.

Section 3.4:

55) According to the general empirical rule, we expect about 50% - 80% of the data to lie within 1 standard deviation of the mean, 90% - 100% of the data to lies within 2 standard deviations of the mean, and 99% - 100% of the data to lie within 3 standard deviations of the mean.

56) A data value is considered to be unusual if it is more than 2 standard deviations away from the mean, and it is considered very unusual if it is more than 3 standard deviations away from the mean.

57) When rounding a z-score, always use exactly 3 decimal places.

58) The expected range for data values is anything that lies within 2 standard deviations of the mean.

59) From exercise (43) we know that $\bar{x} = 1.55$ and $s \approx 0.10453$

a) $\bar{x} - s \approx 1.55 - 0.10453 = 1.44547$
$\bar{x} + s \approx 1.55 + 0.10453 = 1.65453$
$\Rightarrow \dfrac{24}{36} \approx 0.6667 = 66.67\%$

b) $\bar{x} - 2s \approx 1.55 - 2(0.10453) = 1.34094$
$\bar{x} + 2s \approx 1.55 + 2(0.10453) = 1.75906$
$\Rightarrow \dfrac{34}{36} \approx 0.9444 = 94.44\%$

c) $\bar{x} - 3s \approx 1.55 - 3(0.10453) = 1.23641$
$\bar{x} + 3s \approx 1.55 + 3(0.10453) = 1.86359$
$\Rightarrow \dfrac{36}{36} = 100\%$

d) The 66.7% agrees with the 50 - 80% from the empirical rule.
The 94.4% agrees with the 90 - 100% from the empirical rule.
The 100% agrees with the approx. 100% from the empirical rule.

61) a) $z = \dfrac{0.300 - 0.270}{0.053} \approx 0.566$. No, it would not be unusual since it is less than 2 standard deviations above the mean. In fact, since it is less than 1 standard deviation above the mean, this would have been a rather normal batting average for that year.

b) $z = \dfrac{0.400 - 0.270}{0.053} \approx 2.453$. Yes, it would be unusual, because it is more than 2 standard deviations above the mean.

c) $\begin{matrix} \mu - 2\sigma = 0.164 \\ \mu + 2\sigma = 0.376 \end{matrix} \Rightarrow$ Any batting average between 0.164 and 0.376 would NOT be considered unusual. Note: not everything in this range would be considered normal. The lower and upper fourth of this range makes up the gray area.

63) a) $z = \dfrac{97 - 77}{13.207} \approx 1.514$. No, not really, it is less than 2 standard deviations above the mean. It would be considered in the gray area.

b) $z = \dfrac{27 - 77}{13.207} \approx -3.786$. Yes, this would be very unusual as it is more than 3 (almost 4) standard deviation below the mean. Unless thousands of students took this test, there probably would not be a score this low.

c) $\begin{array}{l} \mu - 2\sigma = 50.586 \\ \mu + 2\sigma = 103.414 \end{array} \Rightarrow$ The expected range

for the test scores would be between 50.586 and 103.414. Assuming only whole number scores are possible, then the expected range would be from 51 to 103.

65) $z_1 = \dfrac{0.412 - 0.270}{0.053} \approx 2.679$

$z_2 = \dfrac{100 - 77}{13.207} \approx 1.742$

The 0.412 batting average is the more unusual (rare), and thus impressive, batting average, because it is more standard deviations away from its mean ($z = 2.679$) than the 100 ($z = 1.742$).

67) a) $z = \dfrac{2100 - 1524.6}{235.95} \approx 2.439 \Rightarrow$ Yes, with a z-score of 2.439, this score would be considered unusual since it is more than 2 standard deviations above the mean.

b) No. Such a large number of people take the SAT test every year, it would not be strange to have some of them with combined scores that are more than 2 standard deviations above the mean. These scores would be unusually high due to the low percentage of the time that they occur, yet in a large population, they should still occur.

Section 3.5:

69) P_{12} is called the 12th <u>percentile</u> and it attempts to have 12% of the data set <u>below</u> it.

70) If $L_{Q_1} = 5.75$, then Q_1 is the mean of the <u>5</u>th and <u>6</u>th values in the ordered data set.

71) The IQR is found by taking the difference between Q_3 and Q_1. Graphically, it represents the length of the <u>box</u> in our boxplot.

72) The fences lie $1\frac{1}{2}$ box lengths away from the box. Any values that lie outside the fences are considered possible <u>outliers</u>.

73) An outlier is a value that <u>stands apart</u> from the rest of the data set.

74) The whiskers on a modified boxplot extend to the largest and smallest <u>data values</u> that lie within the <u>fences</u>.

75) Use STAT > SortA(L1) to put the data in order.

a) $L_{P_{43}} = \dfrac{43}{100}(11 + 1) = 5.16 \Rightarrow$

$P_{43} = \dfrac{500 + 520}{2} = 510$

b) $L_{Q_1} = \dfrac{1}{4}(11 + 1) = 3 \Rightarrow Q_1 = 400$

$L_M = \dfrac{1}{2}(11 + 1) = 6 \Rightarrow M = 520$

$L_{Q_3} = \dfrac{3}{4}(11 + 1) = 9 \Rightarrow Q_3 = 560$

5-Num-Sum $= \{260, 400, 520, 560, 660\}$

77) Use STAT > SortA(L1) to put the data in order.

$L_{Q_1} = \dfrac{1}{4}(12 + 1) = 3.25 \Rightarrow$

$Q_1 = \dfrac{134 + 152}{2} = 143$

$L_M = \dfrac{1}{2}(12 + 1) = 6.5 \Rightarrow M = \dfrac{172 + 206}{2} = 189$

$L_{Q_3} = \dfrac{3}{4}(12 + 1) = 9.75 \Rightarrow$

$Q_3 = \dfrac{236 + 263}{2} = 249.5$

5-Num Sum $= \{104, 143, 189, 249.5, 274\}$

79) 5-number summary $\{134, 143, 189, 249.5, 274\}$

$$IQR = 249 - 143 = 106$$

$$\Rightarrow \quad \begin{aligned} LF &= 143 - 1.5 * 106 = -16 \\ UF &= 249.5 + 1.5 * 106 = 408.5 \end{aligned}$$

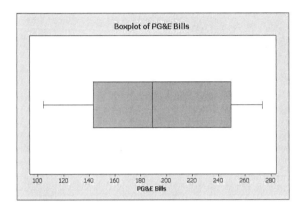

Boxplot of PG&E Bills

Note: No data values past the fences means no possible outliers. You don't need to show the fences if they don't lie within the range of the given data.

81) Sort the data using STAT > SortA(L1)

a) $L_{P_{55}} = \dfrac{55}{100}(23 + 1) = 13.2 \Rightarrow$

$$P_{55} = \dfrac{95 + 96}{2} = 95.5$$

We expect about 55% of the golfers to have scores below 95.5.

Note: We actually have $\dfrac{13}{24} \approx 54.17\%$ of the golfers below 95.5. 55% exactly is not possible with 23 data values.

b) $L_{Q_1} = \dfrac{1}{4}(23 + 1) = 6 \Rightarrow Q_1 = 88$

$$L_M = \dfrac{1}{2}(23 + 1) = 12 \Rightarrow M = 93$$

$$L_{Q_3} = \dfrac{3}{4}(23 + 1) = 18 \Rightarrow Q_3 = 98$$

5-num: $\{71, 88, 93, 98, 106\}$

$$IQR = 98 - 88 = 10 \Rightarrow \begin{aligned} LF &= 88 - 1.5 * 10 = 73 \\ UF &= 98 + 1.5 * 10 = 113 \end{aligned}$$

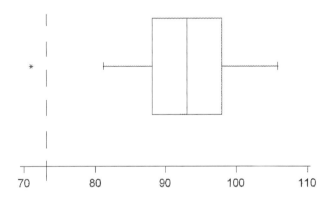

Note: Since 71 is below the lower fence, it is marked as a possible outlier. The left whisker extends to 81, which is the lowest data value within the fences.

83) Sort the data using STAT > SortA(L1)

a) $L_{Q_1} = \dfrac{1}{4}(19+1) = 5 \Rightarrow Q_1 = 30.6$

$L_M = \dfrac{1}{2}(19+1) = 10 \Rightarrow M = 31.5$

$L_{Q_3} = \dfrac{3}{4}(19+1) = 15 \Rightarrow Q_3 = 32.5$

5-num: $\{27.4,\ 30.6,\ 31.5,\ 32.5,\ 33.6\}$

$IQR = 32.5 - 30.6 = 1.9$

$\Rightarrow \begin{array}{l} LF = 30.6 - 1.5*1.9 = 27.75 \\ UF = 32.5 + 1.5*1.9 = 35.35 \end{array}$

Note: 27.4 is a possible outlier because it is below the lower fence. The left-whisker extends to 29.1 because it is the smallest value within the fences.

b) With a sample of size 19, it is hard to be certain of the population shape. If we ignore the outlier, it looks somewhat symmetric and possibly bell shaped. With the outlier, it looks a bit left skewed.

c) Yes, the 27.4 is far below the other values.

d) One possibility is that there was an error in collecting or entering the data. Maybe the mileage is actually higher.
Another possibility is that there is a problem with this car that is hurting its gas mileage.

Chapter Problem:

a) Sort data using STAT > SortA(L1)

$L_{Q_1} = \dfrac{1}{4}(68+1) = 17.25 \Rightarrow Q_1 = 71$

$L_M = \dfrac{1}{2}(68+1) = 34.5 \Rightarrow M = 72$

$L_{Q_3} = \dfrac{3}{4}(68+1) = 51.75 \Rightarrow Q_3 = 75$

5-number summary: $\{47, 71, 72, 75, 80\}$
Note: When the two numbers used to calculate a quartile are the same, the quartile has the same value as the original two numbers.

f) We have the scores for all the golfers, so this is population data. Choose STAT > CALC > 1 Var Stats L1. Remember to change the 47 to 74 first. $\mu \approx 73.03$, $\sigma \approx 2.9153$

g) $283 - 272 = 11 \Rightarrow$ Tiger lost by 11 strokes. He would have needed a final day score that was 11 strokes lower. So he needed to score $72 - 11 = 61$.

h) $z = \dfrac{61 - 73.03}{2.9153} \approx -4.127 \Rightarrow$ Yes, in fact, this would have been very unusual because a score of 61 would have been more than 3 standard deviations below the mean.

i) $\begin{array}{l} \mu - 2\sigma = 67.1994 \\ \mu + 2\sigma = 78.8606 \end{array} \Rightarrow \dfrac{65}{68} \approx 95.59\%$

Note: Since the score of 67 is lower than 67.1994 is would be considered unusual, so it was not counted. All but the 67, 80, and 80 fell in the expected range. This percentage is in line with the General Empirical Rule.

Section 4.1:

1) The standard form of a line in statistics is
$y = b_0 + b_1 x$, where b_0 is the y-intercept and
b_1 is the slope.

2) When the x-value is increased by 1 unit, the
y-value will change by the slope.

3) a) $b_1 = -250 \Rightarrow \dfrac{\Delta v}{\Delta y} = \dfrac{-\$250}{1 yr} \Rightarrow$ For each
additional year of age for these color
copiers, the price decreases by $250.
b) (0 yr, $1500) $\Rightarrow$ New copiers of this type
are worth $1500.
c) Pick any value and substitute into the
equation to find the value of v.

y	v	
1	1250	Plot these 3 points and
2	1000	then connect with a
5	250	straight line.

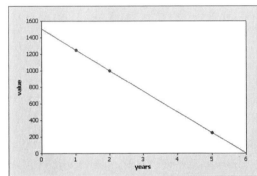

d) This question is not intended to be answered
using the equation. Use the graph to
answer it. Move on the horizontal axis to
3.5 years. From there, move up until you hit
the line. Finally move left to the vertical
axis and note the value. Answers will
vary. Value $\approx$ $625.

5) a) $b_1 = 2.8 \Rightarrow \dfrac{\Delta c}{\Delta w} = \dfrac{\$2.8}{1 lb} \Rightarrow$ For each
additional pound of weight, the cost of
shipping the package increases by $2.80.
b) (0 lb, $21.05) $\Rightarrow$ This formula does not
apply to a weightless package!
c) Even though you can pick any values for w
to input into the equation. It is best to pick
values on the extreme low and high side.

w	c	
1	23.85	Plot these 2 points and
19	74.25	then connect with a
		straight line.

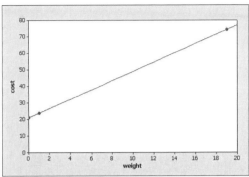

d) Move on the horizontal axis until you reach
the value 7, then move up until you hit the
line. Finally, move to the left until you hit
the vertical axis. Answers will vary.
Value $\approx$ $40.65

7) a) $b_1 = 0.19 \Rightarrow \dfrac{\Delta c}{\Delta m} = \dfrac{\$0.19}{1 mi} \Rightarrow$ For each
additional mile driven, the cost of the
moving van rental increases by $0.19.
b) (0 mi., $29.99) $\Rightarrow$ Before we even put any
miles on the moving van, we already owe
$29.99.
c) Even though you can pick any values for m
to input into the equation. It is best to pick
values that are spread out among the
reasonable possibilities.

m	c	
0	29.99	Plot these 3 points and
100	48.9967.99	then connect with a
200		straight line.

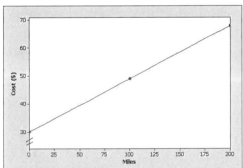

d) Move on the horizontal axis until you reach
the value 70, then move up until you hit the
line. Finally, move to the left until you hit
the vertical axis. Answers will vary.
Approx. $43.29

Section 4.2:

9) The best fitting line for a data set is called the regression line.

10) The best fitting line is the one with the smallest sum of squared errors. An error is the difference between the height of a data point and the height of the line at that same x -value.

11) Linear regression should only be done if a plot of the data values has a roughly linear pattern.

12) When we use a regression equation to make a prediction, we are always predicting the average y-value.

13) It is not wise to make predictions using x-values that are outside of the range of the given data.

14) If the x-value of a data point stands out, then we call it a potentially influential observation. If the y-value of a data point stands out, then we call it an outlier.

15) y stands for the actual y-value of a piece of data. $\bar{y}$ stands for the average of all the y-values in the data set. $\hat{y}$ stands for a predicted y-value using an x-value in the regression equation.

16) When you are given the value of $\sum xy$, use it as a check of data entry in the calculator.

17) a) Line B appears a little closer to more of the points.

b) Line A: Values for $\hat{y}$ are obtained by plugging the x values into the equation given for line A.

x	y	$\hat{y}$	$e^2 = (y - \hat{y})^2$
3	21	18	9
5	25	26	1
6	24	30	36
8	30	38	64
8	41	38	9
11	50	50	0
			$\sum e^2 = 119$

Line B: Values for $\hat{y}$ are obtained by plugging the x values into the equation given for line B.

x	y	$\hat{y}$	$e^2 = (y - \hat{y})^2$
3	21	17.5	12.25
5	25	24.5	0.25
6	24	28	16
8	30	35	25
8	41	35	36
11	50	45.5	20.25
			$\sum e^2 = 109.75$

c) Line B is the better fit because it has a smaller sum of squared error than line A.

19) a) First we make a table to find the needed sums.

x	y	$(x-\bar{x})(y-\bar{y})$	$(x-\bar{x})^2$
3	21	41.528	14.694
5	25	12.528	3.361
6	24	6.528	0.694
8	30	-2.139	1.361
8	41	10.694	1.361
11	50	75.694	17.361
41	191	144.833	38.833

Calculator Tips: You can use the calculator to speed up this process. Enter x-values in L1 and the y-values in L2.
Then let L3 = (L1 – 41/6)(L2 – 191/6).
Then let L4 = (L1 – 41/6)^2.

You can also use LIST >MATH > SUM to assist finding the sums.

Note: The calculator keeps track of more digits than I wrote down in the tables. Using the larger number of decimal places produces more accurate values for b_1 and b_0.

$$b_1 = \frac{\sum(x-\bar{x})(y-\bar{y})}{\sum(x-\bar{x})^2} \approx \frac{144.83333}{38.83333} \approx 3.72962$$

$$b_0 = \bar{y} - b_1\bar{x} \approx \frac{191}{6} - 3.729617 * \frac{41}{6} \approx 6.3476$$

$$\hat{y} \approx 6.3476 + 3.7296x$$

b) Values for $\hat{y}$ are obtained by plugging the x values into the regression equation above.

x	y	$\hat{y}$	$e^2 = (y-\hat{y})^2$
3	21	17.536	11.996
5	25	24.996	0.000
6	24	28.725	22.328
8	30	36.184	38.247
8	41	36.184	23.190
11	50	47.373	6.900
			$\sum e^2 \approx 102.66$

Note: notice that $\sum e^2$ is smaller here than from lines A and B in exercise (17).

21) a) Yes, the data forms a roughly linear pattern.
   b) No, there is no pattern at all to the data.
   c) No, there is a definite pattern, but it is not linear.

23) ae)

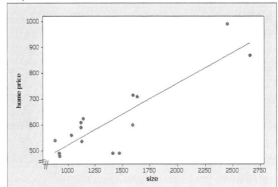

   b) Yes, there is a roughly linear pattern to the data.
   c) Enter the x-values in L1 and the y-values in L2. Choose STAT > CALC > LinReg(a+bx) L1, L2 and we get:
   $\hat{y} \approx 282.74 + 0.239689x$
   Rounding Note: The prices are given in $1000s, so the $100 place is actually the first decimal place. For example, a home that costs $654,300 would be listed as 654.3. So, since we want 1 decimal place in our predictions, we need at least 2 decimal places in our intercept. Since we want 4 digits in our predictions, we need at least 5 digits in our slope.
   d) $\hat{y} \approx 282.74 + 0.239689 * 2200 \approx 810.1$
   $= \$810,100$, yes, 2200 sq ft is within the range of the known home sizes in our data set.
   e) Pick x values near the min and max of the given data values. Plug them into the regression equation.

x	$\hat{y}$	
1000	522.4	Plot these 2 points and
2500	882.0	then connect with a straight line. See line in part (a).

   f) No, 3400 sq ft is larger than any of the homes in our data set.
   g) $\dfrac{\Delta\hat{y}}{\Delta x} = \dfrac{0.240(\$1000)}{1 \text{ ft}^2} = \dfrac{\$240}{1 \text{ ft}^2} \Rightarrow$ For each additional sq ft, the average price of the homes increases by $240.

25) a f)

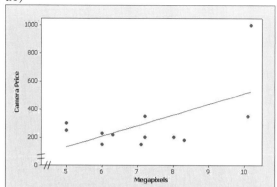

b) No, there does not seem to be a linear pattern to the data.

c) Yes, both (10.2, 1000) and (10.1, 350) seem to be potentially influential observations because they have a lot more mega pixels than the rest of the cameras. In addition, the point (10.2, 1000) would also be an outlier because it seems far too expensive even for the number of mega pixels.

d) Enter the x-values in L1 and the y-values in L2. Choose STAT > CALC > LinReg(a+bx) L1, L2 and we get:
$\hat{y} \approx -251.8 + 76.409x$

Rounding Note: A large prediction rounded to the nearest dollar might be $1234. So, since we want whole numbers for our predictions, we need at least 1 decimal place in our intercept. Since we want 4 digits in our predictions, we need at least 5 digits in our slope.

e) $\hat{y} \approx -251.8 + 76.409 * 9 \approx \$436$, yes and no. Yes because the size of the camera is within the known number of mega pixels in our data set. No because a linear regression wasn't really appropriate on this problem.

f) Pick x values near the min and max of the given data values. Plug them into the regression equation.

x	$\hat{y}$	
5	130	Plot these 2 points and
10	512	then connect with a
		straight line. See line in
		part (a).

g) Yes and no for the same reasons stated in part (d).

h) $b_1 \approx 76.41 \Rightarrow \dfrac{\Delta\hat{y}}{\Delta x} = \dfrac{\$76.41}{1 \text{ mega pixel}} \Rightarrow$ For each additional mega pixel, the average price of digital cameras increases by $76.41.

27) a)

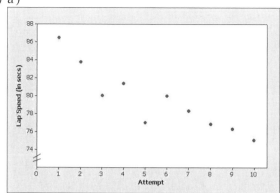

b) Yes, there is a roughly linear pattern to the data set.

c) Not really. (5, 77.05) seems a little low, but not unusually so.

d) Enter the x-values in L1 and the y-values in L2. Choose STAT > CALC > LinReg(a+bx) L1, L2 and we get:
$\hat{y} \approx 85.443 - 1.0739x$

Rounding Note: A large prediction rounded to the nearest hundredth of a second might be 85.22 seconds. So, since we want 2 decimal places for our predictions, we need at least 3 decimal places in our intercept. Since we want 4 digits in our predictions, we need at least 5 digits in our slope.

e) $b_1 \approx -1.0739 \Rightarrow \dfrac{\Delta\hat{y}}{\Delta x} = \dfrac{-1.0739 \text{ sec}}{1 \text{ attempt}} \Rightarrow$

For each additional attempt the lap time drops, on average, about 1.0739 secs.

29) a) Yes, there is a roughly linear pattern to the data set.

b) Enter the x-values (the miles) in L1 and the y-values (the price) in L2. Choose STAT > CALC > LinReg(a+bx) L1, L2 and we get:
$\hat{y} \approx 282.848 - 0.00210945x$

Rounding Note: The prices are given in $100s, so the $1 place is actually the second decimal place. For example, a car that sold for $12,345 would be listed as 123.45. So, since we want 2 decimal places in our predictions, we need at least 3 decimal places in our intercept. Since we want 5 digits in our predictions, we need at least 6 digits in our slope.

c) $\hat{y} \approx 282.848 - 0.00210945 * 35000$

$\approx 209.02 = \$20,902$, yes 35000 is within the range of the known mileages in our data set.

d) No, 120000 miles is more miles than any of the cars in our data set.

e) $b_1 \approx -0.0021 \Rightarrow \dfrac{\Delta\hat{y}}{\Delta x} = \dfrac{-\$0.21}{1 \text{ mile}} \Rightarrow$ For each additional mile, the average price of a mustang GT convertible decreases by $0.21.

f) The car with 25000 miles on it that sold for only $16,900 which is unusually low for so few miles.

g) No cars stand out as potentially influential observations, but the best candidate for this is the one with only 13,759 miles on it. This is a bit lower than any of the cars in our data set.

31) a) Somewhat. There is no clear pattern to the data set, but there is an upward trend that is as much linear as anything else.

b) Enter the x-values in L1 and the y-values in L2. Choose STAT > CALC > LinReg(a+bx) L1, L2 and we get:
$\hat{y} \approx 50.29 + 4.703x$

Rounding Note: A large prediction rounded to the nearest tenth of a point might be 98.5 points. So, since we want 1 decimal places for our predictions, we need at least 2 decimal places in our intercept. Since we want 3 digits in our predictions, we need at least 4 digits in our slope.

c) $\hat{y} \approx 50.29 + 4.703 * 5 \approx 73.8$ points, yes in that 5 points is within the range of the given hw scores. However, the linear pattern is not that strong.

d) Yes. Again 0 points is within the range of the given hw scores.

e) $b_1 \approx 4.7 \Rightarrow \dfrac{\Delta\hat{y}}{\Delta x} = \dfrac{4.7 \text{ Exam Pts}}{1 \text{ Hw pt}} \Rightarrow$ For each additional point scored on the chapter 3 hw assignment, the average exam score is higher by 4.7 points.

33) a) (2000, 500) This is an outlier because the price of $500,000 is unusually low for a 2000 sq foot house. However, it is not a potentially influential observation because the size is within the known home sizes.

b) (4000,1241). This would be a potentially influential observation because it is a much larger home than any in our data set. It is not an outlier because a price of $1,241,000 would follow the linear pattern.

Section 4.3:

35) r^2 is called the coefficient of <u>determination</u>.

36) $\sum(y - \bar{y})^2$ represents the total squared error if we used the <u>average</u> y-value to make our estimates rather than the linear <u>regression</u> equation.

37) $\sum(y - \hat{y})^2$ represents the total squared error if we used the linear <u>regression</u> equation to make predictions.

38) $\dfrac{\sum(y - \bar{y})^2 - \sum(y - \hat{y})^2}{\sum(y - \bar{y})^2}$ represents the <u>percent</u> reduction in squared error when we make predictions by using the x-value in the regression equation rather than just always using the overall average y-value to make our <u>predictions</u>.

39) If r^2 is near 0, then the regression is <u>not useful</u>.

40) If r^2 is near 1, then the regression is <u>very useful</u>.

41) a) $y - \bar{y}$ is represented on the graph by the vertical distance from each data point to the horizontal line. Estimates for each $y - \bar{y}$ are shown on the graph below.

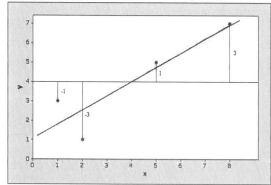

$$\sum(y - \bar{y})^2 = (-1)^2 + (-3)^2 + 1^2 + 3^2 = 20$$

b) $y - \hat{y}$ is represented on the graph by the vertical distance from each data point to the regression line. Estimates for each $y - \hat{y}$ are shown on the graph below.

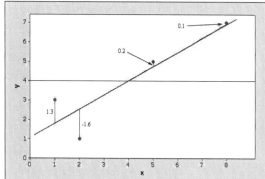

$$\sum(y - \hat{y})^2 \approx 1.3^2 + (-1.6)^2 + 0.2^2 + 0.1^2 = 4.3$$

c) $r^2 = \dfrac{\sum(y - \bar{y})^2 - \sum(y - \hat{y})^2}{\sum(y - \bar{y})^2} \approx \dfrac{20 - 4.3}{20} = 0.785$

43) a) Enter the x-values in L1 and the y-values in L2. Choose STAT > CALC > LinReg(a+bx) L1, L2. If r^2 does not show in the output, see directions for turning "diagnostic on" in section 4.3 of the book. $r^2 \approx 0.7481$

b) We get a 74.81% reduction in squared error when we use the size of the home in the linear regression equation to predict the home price rather than just always using the average home price to make our predictions.

c) 74.81% of the variation in home prices can be explained by using the size of the home in the regression equation.

d) Yes. Removing 74.81% of the squared error would be very useful.

45) a) Enter the x-values in L1 and the y-values in L2. Choose STAT > CALC > LinReg(a+bx) L1, L2. If r^2 does not show in the output, see directions for turning "diagnostic on" in section 4.3 of the book. $r^2 \approx 0.3240$

b) We get a 32.4% reduction in squared error when we use the number of mega pixels in the linear regression equation to predict the price rather than just always using the average price to make our predictions.
OR
32.4% of the variation in price can be explained by using the number of mega pixels in the regression equation.

c) It appears to be somewhat useful in that 32.4% of the squared error is removed. However, most of the upward trend we see can be attributed to the one outlier camera.

47) a) Enter the x-values in L1 and the y-values in L2. Choose STAT > CALC > LinReg(a+bx) L1, L2. If r^2 does not show in the output, see directions for turning "diagnostic on" in section 4.3 of the book. $r^2 \approx 0.8239$

b) We get a 82.39% reduction in squared error when we use the attempt number in the regression equation to predict the lap time rather than just always using the average lap time as our prediction.

c) Yes. Removing 82.39% of the squared error would be very useful.

Section 4.4:

49) r is known as the linear <u>correlation</u> coefficient.

50) If r is close to 1, then there is a <u>strong positive</u> linear correlation between the <u>variables</u> .

51) If r is close to -1, then there is a <u>strong negative</u> linear correlation between the <u>variables</u>.

52) If r is close to 0, then there is <u>weak</u> if any <u>linear</u> correlation between the variables.

53) a) There is an upward pattern to the data, so we should guess a positive values. There is a decent, but not great linear pattern. Answers will vary.

b) Enter the x-values in L1 and the y-values in L2. Choose STAT > CALC > LinReg(a+bx) L1, L2. If r does not show in the output, see directions for turning "diagnostic on" in section 4.3 of the book. $r \approx 0.8649$

c) There is a strong positive linear correlation between the size and price of homes.

55) a) There is a slight upward pattern to the data, so we should guess a positive values. There is a very weak linear pattern. Answers will vary.

b) Enter the x-values in L1 and the y-values in L2. Choose STAT > CALC > LinReg(a+bx) L1, L2. If r does not show in the output, see directions for turning "diagnostic on" in section 4.3 of the book. $r \approx 0.4030$

c) There is a weak moderate positive linear correlation between the chapter 3 hw score and the exam 1 score.

57) a) There is a downward pattern to the data, so we should guess a negative values. There seems to be a pretty strong linear pattern. Answers will vary.

b) Enter the x-values in L1 and the y-values in L2. Choose STAT > CALC > LinReg(a+bx) L1, L2. If r does not show in the output, see directions for turning "diagnostic on" in section 4.3 of the book. $r \approx -0.8792$

c) There is a strong negative linear correlation between the mileage and price of the mustangs.

59) a) There is a downward pattern to the data, so we should guess a negative values. There seems to be a somewhat strong linear pattern. Answers will vary.

b) Enter the x-values in L1 and the y-values in L2. Choose STAT > CALC > LinReg(a+bx) L1, L2. If r does not show in the output, see directions for turning "diagnostic on" in section 4.3 of the book. $r \approx -0.8307$

c) There is a strong negative linear correlation between the ERA and the number of wins for a team.

Chapter Problem:

c)

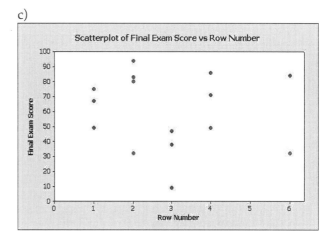

e) Enter the x-values in L1 and the y-values in L2. Choose STAT > CALC > LinReg(a+bx) L1, L2 and we get: $\hat{y} \approx 65.087 - 1.74189x$
Note: No rounding was mentioned in the directions, but this equation should provide predictions reliable to the nearest hundredth, which should be more than adequate.

f) $r \approx -0.1178$ and $r^2 \approx 0.0139$

g) We get a 1.39% reduction in squared error when we use the row number in the linear regression equation to predict the exam score rather than just always using the average exam score to make our predictions.

h) There is weak if any linear correlation between the row number and the final exam scores.

Cumulative Review: Chapters 1 – 4

1) a) CA: $\dfrac{36.55}{46.77} * 750 \approx 586.11 \Rightarrow 586$

WA: $\dfrac{6.47}{46.77} * 750 \approx 103.75 \Rightarrow 104$

OR: $\dfrac{3.75}{46.77} * 750 \approx 60.13 \Rightarrow 60$

586 Californians, 104 Washingtonians, and 60 Oregonians for a total of 750 people.

b) Their position on supporting offshore drilling.

c) Categorical

d) Observational. We are only asking their opinion, not trying to shape it.

e) Inferential. We are trying to use the results of a sample of 750 people to estimate the opinions of 46.77 million people.

2) a) 23.7 years old
    b) Quantitative – Continuous
    c) If I used the ages of those in the lab to try to estimate the average age of all those who attend the college.
    d) If I only used the ages to state the average age of those using the lab.
    e) part (c) would be inferential and part (d) would be descriptive.
    f) Observational. There is no element of design or control, we are simply observing the ages of people who chose on their own to use the lab.

3) The sample was not randomly chosen. The instructor chose his own lab time only. The instructors students are more likely to go to the lab during hours their instructor is there. This will bias the result towards a higher percentage of his students in the overall lab usage.

4) a) All 7 of the people from the population are represented. This is population data.

x	$(x-\mu)^2$
19	34.306
20 *	23.592
22 *	8.163
25 *	0.020
25 *	0.020
28 *	9.878
35	102.878
174	178.859

$$\mu = \frac{174}{7} \approx 24.857 \text{ and}$$

$$\sigma = \sqrt{\frac{\sum(x-\mu)^2}{N}} \approx \sqrt{\frac{178.859}{7}} \approx 5.0548$$

    b) $\mu - \sigma \approx 19.8$ and $\mu + \sigma \approx 29.9 \Rightarrow$
        $\frac{5}{7} \approx 71.43\%$ (See the values marked in the first column of the table above.)

5) We are only seeking to describe this class and we have data from the whole class. Therefore, we are working with population data.
    a) Enter the data into L1, choose STAT > CALC > 1-Var Stats L1 and press ENTER
        $\mu = 70.5$ and $\sigma \approx 20.329$
    b) $\mu - 2\sigma \approx 29.8$ and $\mu + 2\sigma \approx 111.2 \Rightarrow$
        $\frac{36}{38} \approx 94.74\%$

c) Several numbers are repeated, but 76 is repeated the most. The mode is 76

d) Use STAT > EDIT > SortA to put the data in order. $L_{P_{71}} = \frac{71}{100}(38+1) = 27.69$

$$\Rightarrow P_{71} = \frac{81+83}{2} = 82 \Rightarrow \text{ About } 71\% \text{ of}$$

the test scores will be below an 82.

e) $L_{Q_1} = \frac{1}{4}(38+1) = 9.75$

$$\Rightarrow Q_1 = \frac{58+60}{2} = 59$$

$$L_M = \frac{1}{2}(38+1) = 19.5$$

$$\Rightarrow M = \frac{74+76}{2} = 75$$

$$L_{Q_3} = \frac{3}{4}(38+1) = 29.25 \Rightarrow Q_3 = 86$$

Five number summary is {12, 59, 75, 86, 108}.

f) $IQR = 86 - 59 = 27$
    $LF = 59 - 1.5 * 27 = 18.5$
    Therefore, 12 is a possible outlier. The lower whisker extends to 29.

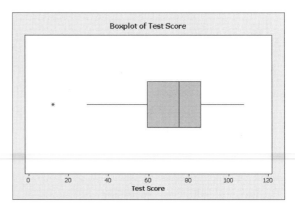

g)

Score	Freq	Rel Freq	Midpts
10 – 19	1	0.0263	14.5
20 – 29	1	0.0263	24.5
30 – 39	1	0.0263	34.5
40 – 49	3	0.0789	44.5
50 – 59	3	0.0789	54.5
60 – 69	7	0.1842	64.5
70 – 79	8	0.2105	74.5
80 – 89	7	0.1842	84.5
90 – 99	6	0.1579	94.5
100 – 109	1	0.0263	104.5
	38	0.9998	

h) Left skewed, the boxplot shows more dispersion and extremes on the left. Also, the mean is much lower than the median.

6) a)

0	79
1	02566778999
2	01356899
3	0000468899
4	1

b)

0	79
1	02
1	566778999
2	013
2	56899
3	00004
3	68899
4	1

c)

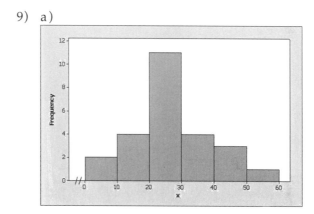

d) The bars almost seem to have random heights in part (b) which seems to make uniform a possibility. However, the dotplot shows more data in the center than on the ends, so perhaps it is a bell-shaped population.

7) a) $z = \dfrac{99-76}{15.3} \approx 1.503 \Rightarrow$ No, 99 is less than 2 standard deviations from the mean.

b) If there are no unusual values, then you expect all values to be between $\mu - 2 \cdot \sigma$ & $\mu + 2 \cdot \sigma$. $\mu - 2\sigma = 45.4$ and $\mu + 2\sigma = 106.6 \Rightarrow$, so the expected range for such a test is from 46 to 106 pts.

Note: I am assuming that the score can only be an integer. I did not round the 45.4 to 46. I used the smaller integer between 45.4 and 106.6. Similarly, 106 is the largest such integer.

c) $z = \dfrac{39-76}{15.3} \approx -2.418 \Rightarrow$ This student is more than 2 standard deviations below the mean. By the Empirical Rule, I expect at least 90% of the data to be within 2 standard deviations. So, at best, this student is in the bottom 10% of the class. It is likely that their situation is worse than this.

8) a) $R = 118 - 19 = 99$

b) If we are simply describing this data set, then it is our population. Using STAT > CALC > 1-Var Stats, we get: $\mu = 67.6$ and $\sigma \approx 30.031$

c) If we are going to use this data to make inferences about a larger population, then this is sample data. Using the calculator we get: $\bar{x} = 67.6$ and $s \approx 31.085$

d) Put the data in order using STAT > EDIT > SortA.

$$L_{Q_1} = \frac{1}{4}(15+1) = 4 \Rightarrow Q_1 = 41$$

$$L_M = \frac{1}{2}(15+1) = 8 \Rightarrow M = 76$$

$$L_{Q_3} = \frac{3}{4}(15+1) = 12 \Rightarrow Q_3 = 94$$

{19, 41, 76, 94, 118}

9) a)

Note: For quantitative data, the bars go from lower cutpoint to lower cutpoint, so there are no gaps. Since zero was moved from its normal spot the double slash mark is needed.

b) Since we are using this data set to make estimates about a larger set, this is sample data. Enter the midpoints into L1. Enter the frequencies in L2. Choose STAT > CALC > 1-Var Stats L1, L2 and press ENTER. $\bar{x} \approx 27$ and $s \approx 12.247$

Note: Since we used midpoints to approximate the actual x-values, are answer are approximations even if we do not round.

10) a)

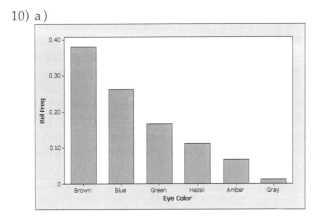

Note: For categorical data, there is no horizontal number line. We simply label each bar. Also, gaps exist between all the bars.

b)

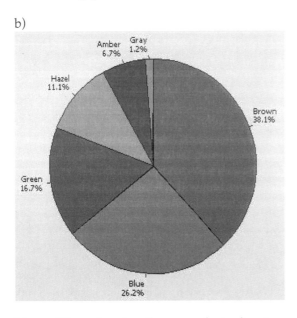

Note: When drawing these graphs by hand, try to take advantage of nice percentages. For example, at 26.2% blue eyes should make up about 1/4 of the graph. If we add together Brown and Hazel, that should be about 1/2 of the graph. The graph above was done on the computer which does not care if the percentages are nice or not.

11) a) Somewhat. There is a very rough linear pattern to the data set.

b) For potentially influential observations, we are look for an x-value, or time, that stands apart from the rest of the data set. (17, 86) This student finished the quiz much faster than any other student.

c) For an outlier we are looking for data points that have y-values that seem unusual for the x-value they are paired with. (29, 47) seems like a pretty low score given the quiz time. (37, 78) seems like a pretty high score given the quiz time. Neither one actually stands apart far enough to be considered obvious outliers.

d) Enter the x-values in L1 and the y-values in L2. Choose STAT > CALC > LinReg(a+bx) L1, L2 and we get:
$$\hat{y} \approx 122.55 - 1.688x$$
Rounding Note: A large prediction rounded to the nearest tenth of a point might be 95.2 points. So, since we want 1 decimal place for our predictions, we need at least 2 decimal places in our intercept. Since we want 3 digits in our predictions, we need at least 4 digits in our slope.

e) Yes, 20 is within the range of the given quiz times. Prediction:
$$\hat{y} \approx 122.55 - 1.688 * 20 \approx 88.8 \text{ points.}$$

f) $b_1 \approx -1.688 \Rightarrow \dfrac{\Delta\hat{y}}{\Delta x} = \dfrac{-1.688 \text{ pts}}{1 \text{ minute}} \Rightarrow$
For each additional minute spent taking the quiz, the average quiz score is about 1.688 points lower.

g) Obtained from the calculator when linear regression is performed. $r \approx -0.6547$, $r^2 \approx 0.4286$

h) We get a 42.86% reduction in squared error when we use the quiz time in the regression equation to predict the quiz score rather than just always using the average overall quiz score as our prediction.

i) There is a reasonably strong negative linear correlation between the quiz time and the quiz score.

j) No for two reasons. First of all this is an observational study. So, even though there is a somewhat strong correlation, that does not prove that longer quiz times cause students to score lower. Secondly, checking the answers should help spot errors and improve the score. The relationship we see is probably the result of the fact that the best prepared students both finish quickly and score high, the least prepared students can't finish quickly and struggle with the material.

12) ad) Just plotting the points is part (a). Adding the line is from part (d).

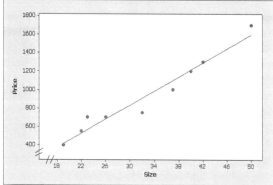

b) Enter the x-values in L1 and the y-values in L2. Choose STAT > CALC > LinReg(a+bx) L1, L2 and we get:

$$\hat{y} \approx -310.381 + 38.12175x$$

Rounding Note: A large prediction rounded to the nearest penny might be $1543.99. So, since we want 2 decimal places for our predictions, we need at least 3 decimal places in our intercept. Since we want 6 digits in our predictions, we need at least 7 digits in our slope.

c) No, 65" is outside of the range of the given TV sizes.

d) Pick x values near the min and max of the given data values. Plug them into the regression equation.

x	$\hat{y}$
20	1595.7
50	452.1

Plot these 2 points and then connect with a straight line. See line in part (a).

e) $b_1 \approx 38.12 \Rightarrow \dfrac{\Delta \hat{y}}{\Delta x} = \dfrac{\$38.12}{1 \text{ inch}} \Rightarrow$ For each additional inch on the size of these TVs, the average price increases by $38.12.

f) From LinReg(a+bx) L1, L2 and we get:

$$r \approx 0.9758 \,,\ r^2 \approx 0.9522$$

g) We get a 95.22% reduction in squared error when we use the TV size in the regression equation to predict the cost rather than just always using the average overall cost as our prediction.

h) There is a very strong positive linear correlation between the size and price of these TVs.

Section 5.1:

1) Classical probability applies to situations where each simple outcome is <u>equally</u> likely to occur.

2) A simple outcome is one that can occur in only <u>one</u> <u>way</u>.

3) Probability = <u>population</u> relative frequency.

4) When we try to interpret probability, we should always think of it as the <u>long</u> term relative frequency.

5) a) $P(Yellow) = \dfrac{12}{87} \approx 0.1379$

b) $P(Orange) = \dfrac{17}{87} \approx 0.1954$

c) It is often easier to subtract what you don't want from the total rather than counting what you do want.

$$P(Not\ Green) = \dfrac{87-14}{87} \approx 0.8391$$

7) Population relative frequencies have the same value as the corresponding probabilities. So, we can just use the relative frequencies that are given to answer these questions.

a) $P(Soph) = 0.2730$

b) $P(Senior) = 0.1974$

c) For this one, it is easier to subtract away the probability of the event we do not want to occur from the total probability of 1.

$P(not\ Freshman) = 1 - 0.2954 = 0.7046$

9) a) $P(A) = \dfrac{1}{6} \approx 0.1667$

b) $P(B) = P(\{1,3,5\}) = \dfrac{3}{6} = 0.5$

c) $P(C) = P(\{3,4,5,6\}) = \dfrac{4}{6} \approx 0.6667$

d) $P(not\ A) = P(\{1,2,3,5,6\}) = \dfrac{5}{6} \approx 0.8333$

e) In the long run, about 66.67% of the rolls will be greater or equal to 3.

11) a) $P(A2) = \dfrac{4193}{8995} \approx 0.4661$

b) $P(B4) = \dfrac{870}{8995} \approx 0.0967$

c) $P(not\ A1) = \dfrac{8995-3919}{8995} \approx 0.5643$

13) We should begin this problem by making a chart for all of the possible sums when two dice are rolled.

	1	2	3	4	5	6
1	2	3	4	5	6	7
2	3	4	5	6	7	8
3	4	5	6	7	8	9
4	5	6	7	8	9	10
5	6	7	8	9	10	11
6	7	8	9	10	11	12

a) The chart reveals that 36 of the possible combinations of the dice result in a sum of 5.

$$P(\text{Sum is 5}) = \dfrac{4}{36} \approx 0.1111$$

b) $P(\text{Sum} > 7) = P(Sum \in \{8,9,10,11,12\})$

$$= \dfrac{5+4+3+2+1}{36} \approx 0.4167$$

c) Doubles means that both of the dice are the same. We can list the outcomes as an ordered pair. For example, double 3's could be written as (3, 3). So we get:

$P(Doubles) =$

$P(\{(1,1),(2,2),(3,3),(4,4),(5,5),(6,6)\})$

$$= \dfrac{6}{36} \approx 0.1667$$

d) For this one, the two numbers don't need to be the same. They just both need to be odd.

$$P(\text{Both Odd}) = P\left(\begin{Bmatrix} (1,1),(1,3),(1,5) \\ (3,1),(3,3),(3,5) \\ (5,1),(5,3),(5,5) \end{Bmatrix}\right)$$

$$= \dfrac{9}{36} = 0.25$$

Section 5.2:

15) If two events can not occur simultaneously, then they are <u>mutually</u> <u>exclusive</u> .

16) Visually, we think of an 'AND' as the <u>overlap</u> of two events.

17) For an 'OR' event to occur, <u>a t</u> <u>least</u> one of the listed events must occur.

18) The special addition rule can only be used if the events are <u>mutually</u> <u>exclusive</u> .

19) a) The phrasing here indicates that we want the person selected to have both of the indicated qualities. That means that this is an AND statement. To find AND probabilities from a table like this, you just need to find the overlap between the indicated row and column.

$$P(\text{A1 \& B4}) = \frac{375}{8995} \approx 0.0417$$

b) This time the language indicated that we are finding A2 OR B3. To compute an OR probability in such a table, count all the values from the first event and add in any NEW values from the other event. See the table below.

	Dem A1	Rep A2	Other A3	Total
0 - < $25K B1	805	873	168	1846
$25K - < $50K B2	1562	1611	370	3543
$50K - < $100K B3	1177	1284	275	2736
$100K+ B4	375	425	70	870
Total	3919	4193	883	8995

You can see that I circled all the items from A2 and then the new stuff from B3. We know add all circled contents.

$$P(\text{A2 or B3}) = \frac{4193 + 1177 + 275}{8995} \approx 0.6276$$

c) This time we want items that are NOT A3 AND are in B1. See the chart below.

	Dem A1	Rep A2	Other A3	Total
0 - < $25K B1	805	873	168	1846
$25K - < $50K B2	1562	1611	370	3543
$50K - < $100K B3	1177	1284	275	2736
$100K+ B4	375	425	70	870
Total	3919	4193	883	8995

The items that are not A3 have been boxed. The items that are B1 have been circled. We want the two cells in the overlap.

$$P\big((\text{not A3}) \, \& \, \text{B1}\big) = \frac{805 + 873}{8995} \approx 0.1865$$

d) Events A & B are mutually exclusive iff $P(\text{A \& B}) = 0$.

$$P(\text{A2 \& B1}) = \frac{873}{8995} \neq 0 \Rightarrow \text{No, A2 and}$$

B1 are not mutually exclusive.

21) a) $A = \{5\}$, $B = \{0,1,2,3,4\}$, $C = \{3,4,5\}$, $D = \{0,1,2\}$. It would be useful to write these out like this even if the problem did not ask us to.

b) Mutually exclusive pair groups have no overlapping elements at all. The mutually exclusive pairs are A&B , A&D , C&D. There are no larger mutually exclusive groups in this problem.

c) 'AND' means overlap, so we look to see what elements these events have in common.

$$P(\text{B \& C}) = P(\{3,4\}) = \frac{13 + 14}{44} \approx 0.6136$$

d) For an 'OR' problems, take all the elements of the first event {0,1,2,3,4} and also anything new from the second event {5}.

$$P(\text{B or C}) = P(\{0,1,2,3,4,5\}) = \frac{44}{44} = 1$$

e) The overlapping elements from B and D are
    {0,1,2}. Because D is completely contained
    in B, the overlap is D.

$$P(\text{B \& D}) = P(\{0,1,2\}) = \frac{1+1+5}{44} \approx 0.1591$$

f) For an 'OR', we would normally take
    everything from B and anything new from
    D. But D has nothing new to offer. So, in
    this case, B or D = B.

$$P(\text{B or D}) = P(\{0,1,2,3,4\}) = \frac{44-10}{44} \approx 0.7727$$

g) $P(\text{A or (not C)}) = P(\{5\} \text{ or } \{0,1,2\}) =$

$$\frac{10+1+1+5}{44} \approx 0.3864$$

23) a) $P(\text{Red or Blue}) = \dfrac{10+23}{87} \approx 0.3793$

b) $P(\text{Green or Orange}) = \dfrac{14+17}{87} \approx 0.3563$

c) None of the m&m's are more than 1 color.

$$P(\text{Brown \& Yellow}) = \frac{0}{87} = 0$$

25) In problems involving the results of rolling two
    dice, it is helpful to look at the chart of all
    possible outcomes.

	1	2	3	4	5	6
1	2	3	4	5	6	7
2	3	4	5	6	7	8
3	4	5	6	7	8	9
4	5	6	7	8	9	10
5	6	7	8	9	10	11
6	7	8	9	10	11	12

a) Since this is an 'OR', first I would count all
    the even sums. There are 18 of these. Then
    I would count all of the sums greater than 9
    that are not even. This would just be the
    two rolls resulting in a sum of 11. Then I put
    these all together.

$$P(\text{sum is even or sum} > 9) = \frac{18+2}{36} \approx 0.5556$$

b) For the 'AND', I only want rolls that
    resulted in both an even sum and a sum > 9.

$$P(\text{sum is even \& sum} > 9) =$$

$$P(\text{sum} \in \{10,12\}) = \frac{3+1}{36} \approx 0.1111$$

c) For this one, I would count all the sums less
    than six and then also count any doubles, I
    did not have yet.

$$P(\text{sum} < 6 \text{ or doubles}) =$$

$$P(\text{sum} \in \{2,3,4,5\},(3,3),(4,4),(5,5),(6,6))$$

$$= \frac{1+2+3+4+4}{36} \approx 0.3889$$

Note: double 1s and double 2s were already
counted in the sum is 2 or the sum is 4. We
don't want to double count when doing an
'OR' problem.

d) This time, we just want the overlap which
    is the two rolls just discussed. (1,1) and
    (2,2) are both doubles and have sums less
    than 6.

$$P(\text{sum} < 6 \text{ \& doubles}) =$$

$$P(\{(1,1),(2,2)\}) = \frac{2}{36} \approx 0.0556$$

27) For alphabet problems such as these, we simply
    rely on probability formulas.

a) $P(\text{A or B}) = P(A) + P(B) - P(A \& B)$
    $= 0.3425 + 0.5283 - 0.2367 = 0.6341$

b) $P(\text{not } A) = 1 - P(A) = 1 - 0.3425 = 0.6575$

c) No, $P(A \& B) \neq 0$. For two events to be
    mutually exclusive, the probability of
    their overlap must be zero.

29) We have seen 8 cards, so 44 remain possibilities
    for the river card. We have seen no 6's and no
    Jacks, so 4 of each remain in the deck.

$$P(6 \text{ or Jack}) = \frac{4+4}{44} \approx 0.1818$$

31) a) We have already seen two 9's and two 10's,
    so only 2 of each exist in the 44 remaining
    unseen cards.

$$P(6 \text{ or } 10) = \frac{2+2}{44} \approx 0.0909$$

b) We have already seen 4 of the 13 spades in
    the deck, so 9 of the remaining 44 cards are
    spades.

$$P(\text{spade}) = \frac{13-4}{44} \approx 0.2045$$

c) We can only win as described in parts (a)
    and (b) and these are mutually exclusive
    possibilities, so we just add the results.

$$P(\text{win}) = \frac{4}{44} + \frac{9}{44} \approx 0.2955$$

Section 5.3:

33) When you do a conditional probability problem, the given becomes the new <u>sample space</u>.

34) If two events are independent, then one event occurring doesn't <u>affect</u> whether or not the other one will occur.

35) a) This is not a conditional probability question. Therefore, we use the grand total for the denominator and the total number of democrats for the numerator.

$$P(A1) = \frac{3919}{8995} \approx 0.4357$$

b) This time B1 is the given, so it become our new sample space. It as if the table only contained the following info.

	Dem A1	Rep A2	Other A3	Total
0 - < $25K B1	805	873	168	1846

$$P(A1|B1) = \frac{805}{1846} \approx 0.4361$$

c) No, $P(A1|B1) \neq P(A1)$. It is true that they are not independent because the two probabilities are not exactly equal. However, the difference is very small, so they two variables only have a minor effect on one another.

d) We need to see if conditional probability is different than an individual probability for these two variables. We will compare $P(A2)$ to $P(A2|B4)$.

$$P(A2) = \frac{4193}{8995} \approx 0.4661$$

	Dem A1	Rep A2	Other A3	Total
$100K+ B4	375	425	70	870

$$P(A2|B4) = \frac{425}{870} \approx 0.4885$$

Since $P(A2|B4) \neq P(A2)$, A2 and B4 are not independent of each other.

37) **Note**: $A = \{5\}$, $B = \{0,1,2,3,4\}$, $C = \{3,4,5\}$, $D = \{0,1,2\}$.

a) The sample space is reduced to the given B.

Hw Score	0	1	2	3	4	
Frequency	1	1	5	13	14	

$$P(D|B) = \frac{7}{34} \approx 0.2059$$

b) This time the sample space is reduced to the event D.

Hw Score	0	1	2	
Frequency	1	1	5	

We can only count the parts of B that exist in the new sample space.

$$P(B|D) = \frac{7}{7} = 1$$

c) Once again, the sample space is reduced to the given B.

Hw Score	0	1	2	3	4	
Frequency	1	1	5	13	14	

We count the parts of C that exist in this new reduced sample space.

$$P(C|B) = \frac{13+14}{34} \approx 0.7941$$

d) This time the sample space is reduced to the given C.

Hw Score	0	1	2	3	4	5
Frequency	1	1	5	13	14	10

We can only count the part of B that exists in this new reduced sample space.

$$P(B|C) = \frac{13+14}{37} \approx 0.7297$$

e) $P(C) = \frac{37}{44} \approx 0.8409 \Rightarrow$ NO, $P(C|B) \neq P(C)$

f) $P(A \& D) = P(\{5\} \& \{0,1,2\}) = \dfrac{0}{44} = 0$

The events have no overlap.

Yes, since $P(A \& D) = 0$.

g) $P(A) = \dfrac{10}{44} \approx 0.2273$,

$P(A|D) = 0 \Rightarrow P(A|D) \neq P(A)$

So, no they are not independent.

39) a) $P(R1 \& Y2) = P(R1)P(Y2|R1) =$

$\dfrac{10}{87} * \dfrac{12}{86} \approx 0.0160$

b) $P(G1 \& G2) = P(G1)P(G2|G1) =$

$\dfrac{14}{87} * \dfrac{13}{86} \approx 0.0243$

c) $P(Br \& Bl) = P\big((Br_1 \& Bl_2) \text{ or } (Bl_1 \& Br_2)\big)$

$= \dfrac{11}{87} * \dfrac{23}{86} + \dfrac{23}{87} * \dfrac{11}{86} \approx 0.0676$

d) $P(Or_1 \& Or_2 \& Or_3 \& Or_4) =$

$\dfrac{17}{87} * \dfrac{16}{86} * \dfrac{15}{85} * \dfrac{14}{84} \approx 0.0011$

41) This is an alphabet problem, so we will simply solve it by applying the appropriate formulas.

a) $P(A|B) = \dfrac{P(A \& B)}{P(B)} = \dfrac{0.222}{0.388} \approx 0.5722$

b) $P(B|A) = \dfrac{P(A \& B)}{P(A)} = \dfrac{0.222}{0.415} \approx 0.5349$

c) No, $P(A|B) \neq P(A)$

43) This is an alphabet problem, so we will simply solve it by applying the appropriate formulas.

a) Because the problem states that A and B are independent events, we can use the special multiplication rule.

$P(A \& B) = P(A)P(B) =$

$0.3891 * 0.6742 \approx 0.2623$

b) No, $P(A \& B) \neq 0$

c) $P(A \& B) = 0 \Rightarrow P(A|B) = \dfrac{P(A \& B)}{P(B)} = 0$,

so unless $P(A) = 0$, they will not be independent!

45) The rolls of a die should be independent of one another. So, we can use the special multiplication rule when doing these problems.

a) $P(6 \text{ on all 4 rolls}) =$

$P(6_1) * P(6_2) * P(6_3) * P(6_4) = \left(\dfrac{1}{6}\right)^4$

$\approx 0.0007716 \approx 0.0008$

b) $P(\text{same number on all rolls}) =$

$P(\text{All 1's or All 2's or } \dots \text{ or All 6's}) =$

$\left(\dfrac{1}{6}\right)^4 + \left(\dfrac{1}{6}\right)^4 + \left(\dfrac{1}{6}\right)^4 + \left(\dfrac{1}{6}\right)^4 + \left(\dfrac{1}{6}\right)^4 + \left(\dfrac{1}{6}\right)^4$

$= 6 * \left(\dfrac{1}{6}\right)^4 \approx 0.0046$

47) We have seen 7 cards, so 45 remain unseen.

a) We have seen 2 fives, so 2 remain unseen.

$P(5_{turn} \& 5_{river}) = \dfrac{2}{45} * \dfrac{1}{44} \approx 0.0010$

b) We have only seen 1 Ace, so 3 remain.

$P(A_{turn} \& A_{river}) = \dfrac{3}{45} * \dfrac{2}{44} \approx 0.0030$

c) We have seen no Kings or Queens, so all 4 of each remain possible. It doesn't matter which one comes first, so we will consider both orders.

$P\big((K_{turn} \& Q_{river}) \text{ or } (Q_{turn} \& K_{river})\big)$

$= \dfrac{4}{45} * \dfrac{4}{44} + \dfrac{4}{45} * \dfrac{4}{44} \approx 0.0162$

d) We have computed all three ways we could win. These ways are mutually exclusive, so we just add them together.

$P(winning) =$

$\dfrac{2}{45} * \dfrac{1}{44} + \dfrac{3}{45} * \dfrac{2}{44} + \dfrac{4}{45} * \dfrac{4}{44} + \dfrac{4}{45} * \dfrac{4}{44}$

≈ 0.0202

Section 5.4:

49) A random variable is a numerical quantity whose value depends on <u>chance</u>.

50) When we are asked to find the probability distribution for a discrete random variable, we should make a <u>chart</u> that lists the possible values of the variable together with their <u>probabilities</u>.

51) The hint says to make a chart like for dice, so we should begin by making that chart. Possibilities from the left pocket are shown down the left side, the possibilities from the right are on top, and the possible sums make up the body of the table.

	1	1	2	3	5
1	2	2	3	4	6
2	3	3	4	5	7
3	4	4	5	6	8
5	6	6	7	8	10

a) We now see that there are 20 possible combinations, so our denominator will always be 20. We then count each possible sum's frequency for the numerator. For example: $P(X=6) = \dfrac{4}{20} = 0.20$.

x	P(x)
2	0.10
3	0.15
4	0.20
5	0.10
6	0.20
7	0.10
8	0.10
10	0.05

b) The complete histogram is shown below followed by a few notes.

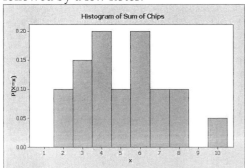

Histogram of Sum of Chips

Notes: Probability is the same as population relative frequency. Therefore, this histogram is almost the same as a relative frequency histogram. We simply label the vertical axis as probability. Also, this is single value grouping, so the bars go from 1/2 mark to 1/2 mark.

53) The probabilities for single values are all shown in the chart, so we simply use these to answer the questions.

a) $P(X=9) = 0.2927$

b) $P(X \geq 6) = 0.1707 + 0.1463 + 0.1463 + 0.2927 + 0.0732 = 0.8292$

c) $P(X < 5) = 0.0488 + 0.0244 + 0 + 0 = 0.0732$

d) $P(5 \leq X < 9) = 0.0976 + 0.1707 + 0.1463 + 0.1463 = 0.5609$

e) For this one, we will use the conditional probability rule.

$$P(X < 7 | X \geq 5) = \frac{P(X < 7 \,\&\, X \geq 5)}{P(X \geq 5)} =$$

$$\frac{P(X = 5 \text{ or } X = 6)}{P(X \geq 5)} = \frac{0.0976 + 0.1707}{1 - 0.0488 - 0.0244}$$

$$\approx 0.2895$$

55) The probabilities for single values are all shown in the chart, so we simply use these to answer the questions.

a) $P(X=2) = 0.1760$

b) $P(X \geq 1) = 1 - P(X = 0) = 1 - 0.3798 = 0.6202$

c) $P(X < 4) = 1 - P(X \geq 4) = 1 - 0.0073 - 0.0007 = 0.9920$

d) $P(1 \leq X < 5) = 0.3909 + 0.1760 + 0.0453 + 0.0073 = 0.6195$

e) For this one, we will use the conditional probability rule.

$$P(X = 1 | X \geq 1) = \frac{P(X = 1 \,\&\, X \geq 1)}{P(X \geq 1)} =$$

$$\frac{P(X = 1)}{P(X \geq 1)} = \frac{0.3909}{1 - 0.3798} \approx 0.6303$$

f) Start adding the probabilities from the bottom of the chart up until you reach the desired total.

$0 + 0 + 0 + 0.0007 + 0.0073 + 0.0453 + 0.1760 = 0.2293 \Rightarrow k = 2$

g) If we include the probabilities for 0 and 1, then our total will be too big. If we leave them both out, our total will be too small. Therefore, start with 1 and keep adding until we get the desired total.

$0.3909 + 0.1760 + 0.0453 = 0.6122 \Rightarrow j = 1, k = 3$

Section 5.5:

57) The mean of a random variable is also called the <u>expected</u> value.

58) μ_x and σ_x tell us the expected mean and standard deviation after a <u>large</u> number of trials.

59) a) $\mu_x = \sum xP(x)$, so we will make a table to get the needed sum. **Calculator Tip:** Enter the x 's in L1 and the $P(x)$'s in L2, then let L3 = L1*L2

x	$P(x)$	$xP(x)$
2	0.10	0.20
3	0.15	0.45
4	0.20	0.80
5	0.10	0.50
6	0.20	1.20
7	0.10	0.70
8	0.10	0.80
10	0.05	0.50
		5.15

$\mu_x = \sum xP(x) = 5.15$

b) After repeating this chip selection process many times, we expect the average of the sums obtained to be about $5.15.

c) $\sigma_x = \sqrt{\sum (x - \mu_x)^2 P(x)}$, so we need to add a $(x - \mu_x)^2 P(x)$ column to our table. **Calculator Tip:** Let L4 = (L1 – 5.15)^2*L2

x	$P(x)$	$xP(x)$	$(x - \mu_x)^2 P(x)$
2	0.10	0.20	0.992250
3	0.15	0.45	0.693375
4	0.20	0.80	0.264500
5	0.10	0.50	0.002250
6	0.20	1.20	0.144500
7	0.10	0.70	0.342250
8	0.10	0.80	0.812250
10	0.05	0.50	1.176125
		5.15	4.4275

$\sigma_x = \sqrt{\sum (x - \mu_x)^2 P(x)} = \sqrt{4.4275} \approx 2.1042$

d) $P(\mu_x - \sigma_x < X < \mu_x + \sigma_x) =$
$P(5.15 - 2.1042 < X < 5.15 + 2.1042) =$
$P(3.0458 < X < 7.2542) = P(4 \le X \le 7)$
$= 0.20 + 0.10 + 0.20 + 0.10 = 0.60$

e) $P(\mu_x - 2\sigma_x < X < \mu_x + 2\sigma_x) =$
$P(5.15 - 2 * 2.1042 < X < 5.15 + 2 * 2.1042)$
$P(0.9416 < X < 9.3584) =$
$P(2 \le X \le 8) = 1 - 0.05 = 0.95$

61) a) $\mu_x = \sum xP(x)$, so we will make a table to get the needed sum. **Calculator Tip:** Enter the x 's in L1 and the $P(x)$'s in L2, then let L3 = L1*L2

x	$P(x)$	$xP(x)$
1	0.0488	0.0488
2	0.0244	0.0488
3	0	0
4	0	0
5	0.0976	0.488
6	0.1707	1.0242
7	0.1463	1.0241
8	0.1463	1.1704
9	0.2927	2.6343
10	0.0732	0.732
		7.1706

$\mu_x = \sum xP(x) = 7.1706$

b) $\sigma_x = \sqrt{\sum (x - \mu_x)^2 P(x)}$, so we need to add a $(x - \mu_x)^2 P(x)$ column to our table. **Calculator Tip:** Let L4 = (L1 – 7.1706)^2*L2

x	$P(x)$	$xP(x)$	$(x - \mu_x)^2 P(x)$
1	0.0488	0.0488	1.85812
2	0.0244	0.0488	0.65234
3	0	0	0
4	0	0	0
5	0.0976	0.488	0.45984
6	0.1707	1.0242	0.23391
7	0.1463	1.0241	0.00426
8	0.1463	1.1704	0.10064
9	0.2927	2.6343	0.97958
10	0.0732	0.732	0.58600
		7.1706	4.8747

$\sigma_x = \sqrt{\sum (x - \mu_x)^2 P(x)} = \sqrt{4.8747} \approx 2.2079$

c) $z = \dfrac{2 - 7.1706}{2.2079} \approx -2.342 \Rightarrow$ Yes, a rating of 2 would be more than 2 standard deviations below the mean.

d) $\mu_x - 2\sigma_x = 2.7548$ and $\mu_x + 2\sigma_x = 11.5864 \Rightarrow$ Anywhere from 3 to 10 is expected for the rating.

63) a) $\mu_x = \sum xP(x)$, so we will make a table to get the needed sum. **Calculator Tip**: Enter the x's in L1 and the $P(x)$'s in L2, then let L3 = L1*L2

x	$P(x)$	$xP(x)$
0	0.3798	0
1	0.3909	0.3909
2	0.1760	0.352
3	0.0453	0.1359
4	0.0073	0.0292
5	0.0007	0.0035
6	0.0000	0
7	0.0000	0
8	0.0000	0
		0.9115

$\mu_x = \sum xP(x) = 0.9115$

b) $\sigma_x = \sqrt{\sum (x-\mu_x)^2 P(x)}$, so we need to add a $(x-\mu_x)^2 P(x)$ column to our table. **Calculator Tip**: Let L4 = (L1 – 0.9115)^2*L2

x	$P(x)$	$xP(x)$	$(x-\mu_x)^2 P(x)$
0	0.3798	0	0.31555
1	0.3909	0.3909	0.00306
2	0.1760	0.352	0.20853
3	0.0453	0.1359	0.19759
4	0.0073	0.0292	0.06963
5	0.0007	0.0035	0.01170
6	0.0000	0	0
7	0.0000	0	0
8	0.0000	0	0
		0.9115	0.80606

$\sigma_x = \sqrt{\sum (x-\mu_x)^2 P(x)} = \sqrt{0.80606} \approx 0.89781$

c) $z = \dfrac{3-0.9115}{0.89781} \approx 2.326 \Rightarrow$ Yes, winning 3 would be unusual because it is more that 2 standard deviations away from the mean.

d) $\mu_x - 2\sigma_x = -0.88412$ and $\mu_x + 2\sigma_x = 2.70712 \Rightarrow$ Anywhere from 0 to 2 winning tickets is expected.

Section 5.6:

65) $\binom{n}{x}$ represents the number of ways of <u>choosing</u> x objects from a set of n objects.

66) An n, p, q problem is officially known as having the <u>binomial</u> distribution. These problems are about counting the number of <u>successes</u> in many trials.

67) For combinations, you need to choose MATH > PROB > nCr on the calculator.

a) $\binom{9}{3} = 84$

b) $\binom{9}{6} = 84$

c) $\binom{15}{4} = 1365$

d) $\binom{15}{11} = 1365$

69) Handshakes happen between groups of 2. So we need to know the number of groups of 2 possible among 20 people. $\binom{20}{2} = 190$ handshakes.

71) a) The possible outcomes are:

HHH	HHT	HTH	THH	HTT	THT	TTH	TTT

b) The outcomes of coin tosses are independent of each other, so we can use the special multiplication rule to find the probabilities.

Outcomes	Probability
HHH	$0.5*0.5*0.5 = 0.125$
HHT	$0.5*0.5*0.5 = 0.125$
HTH	$0.5*0.5*0.5 = 0.125$
THH	$0.5*0.5*0.5 = 0.125$
HTT	$0.5*0.5*0.5 = 0.125$
THT	$0.5*0.5*0.5 = 0.125$
TTH	$0.5*0.5*0.5 = 0.125$
TTT	$0.5*0.5*0.5 = 0.125$

c) $P(H_1 \,\&\, H_2 \,\&\, T_3) = 0.5*0.5*0.5 = 0.125$

d) Since no order is specified, we must consider all possible orders of 2 heads and a tail and add up all their probabilities.

$P(2 \text{ heads } \& 1 \text{ tail}) =$

$P(HHT \text{ or } HTH \text{ or } THH) =$

$0.125 + 0.125 + 0.125 = 3*0.125 = 0.375$

e) $P(X=0) = P(TTT) = (0.5)^3 = 0.125$

$P(X=1) = P(HTT \text{ or } THT \text{ or } TTH)$

$= 3*(0.5)^3 = 0.375$

$P(X=2) = P(HHT \text{ or } HTH \text{ or } THH)$

$= 3*(0.5)^3 = 0.375$

$P(X=3) = P(HHH) = (0.5)^3 = 0.125$

x	0	1	2	3
P(x)	0.125	0.375	0.375	0.125

f) We need to make a table to get the needed sums.

x	$P(x)$	$xP(x)$	$(x-\mu_x)^2 P(x)$
0	0.125	0	0.28125
1	0.375	0.375	0.09375
2	0.375	0.750	0.09375
3	0.125	0.375	0.28125
		1.5	0.75

$\mu_x = \sum xP(x) = 1.5$ and

$\sigma_x = \sqrt{\sum (x-\mu_x)^2 P(x)} = \sqrt{0.75} \approx 0.86603$

73) a) $n=3, p=0.5, q=0.5$

b) $P(X=0) = q^3 = (0.5)^3 = 0.125$

$P(X=1) = \binom{3}{1}(0.5)(0.5)^2 = 0.375$

$P(X=2) = \binom{3}{2}(0.5)^2(0.5) = 0.375$

$P(X=3) = p^3 = (0.5)^3 = 0.125$

x	0	1	2	3
P(x)	0.125	0.375	0.375	0.125

c) $\mu_x = np = 3*0.5 = 1.5$,

$\sigma_x = \sqrt{npq} = \sqrt{3*0.5*0.5} \approx 0.86603$

75) $n=6, p=0.73 \Rightarrow q=1-0.73=0.27$

Note: This is a binomial distribution, so I will find all probabilities using the binomial probability formula.

a) $P(X=4) = \binom{6}{4}(0.73)^4(0.27)^2 \approx 0.3105$

On a graphing calculator, this is entered as:

```
6 nCr 4*0.73^4*0
.27^2
         .3105347653
```

b) **Calculator tip**: Obtain the remaining probabilities by using 2ND ENTER and then editing the previous calculator entry. Or you can enter the x's in L1 and then let L2 = 6 nCr L1*0.73^L1*0.27^(6-L1)

x	$P(x)$
0	0.0004
1	0.0063
2	0.0425
3	0.1531
4	0.3105
5	0.3358
6	0.1513

c) $\mu_x = np = 6*0.73 = 4.38$,

$\sigma_x = \sqrt{npq} = \sqrt{6*0.73*0.27} \approx 1.0875$

77) a) $n=8, p=0.6, q=1-0.6=0.4$

b) $P(X=5) = \binom{8}{5}(0.6)^5(0.4)^3 \approx 0.2787$

```
8 nCr 5*0.6^5*0.
4^3
         .27869184
```

c) For this one, the order was specified, so we don't need the combination to count the number of ways it could occur. It can only occur one way, 5 successes followed by 3 failures. So, we get:

$(0.6)^5(0.4)^3 \approx 0.0050$

d) **Calculator tip**: Obtain the remaining probabilities by using 2ND ENTER and then editing the previous calculator entry. Or you can enter the x's in L1 and then let L2 = 8 nCr L1*0.6^L1*0.4^(8-L1)

x	$P(x)$
0	0.0007
1	0.0079
2	0.0413
3	0.1239
4	0.2322
5	0.2787
6	0.2090
7	0.0896
8	0.0168

e) $\mu_x = np = 8*0.6 = 4.8$,

$\sigma_x = \sqrt{npq} = \sqrt{8*0.6*0.4} \approx 1.3856$

79) $n = 25$, $p = 0.625$, $q = 1 - p = 0.375$

a) $P(X = 12) = \binom{25}{12}(0.625)^{12}(0.375)^{13} \approx 0.0536$

```
25 nCr 12*0.625^
12*0.375^13
         .0535790596
```

b) **Calculator tip**: Obtain the remaining probabilities by using 2ND ENTER and then editing the previous calculator entry. Or you can enter the x's you need in L1 and then let L2 = 25 nCr L1*0.625^L1*0.375^(25-L1). We then add together the values.

$P(11 \leq X < 15) = P(11) + P(12) + P(13) + P(14)$
$\approx 0.0276 + 0.0536 + 0.0893 + 0.1276$
$= 0.2981$

c) $P(X \leq 22) = 1 - P(23) - P(24) - P(25)$
$\approx 1 - 0.0009 - 0.0001 - 0.0000 = 0.9990$

d) $\mu_x = np = 25 * 0.625 = 15.625$, if we repeatedly selected 25 students and counted the number of females each time, in the long run, the average number of females would be around 15.625.

e) $\sigma_x = \sqrt{npq} = \sqrt{25 * 0.625 * 0.375} \approx 2.4206$

f) $z = \dfrac{20 - 15.625}{2.4206} \approx 1.807 \Rightarrow$ not really, 20 females would be less than 2 standard deviations above the mean.

g) $\mu_x - 2\sigma_x \approx 10.78$ and $\mu_x + 2\sigma_x \approx 20.47 \Rightarrow$ Anywhere from 11 to 20 females.

81) $n = 10$, $p = 0.768$, $q = 1 - p = 0.232$

a) $P(X \geq 8) = P(8) + P(9) + P(10) \approx$
$0.2931 + 0.2156 + 0.0714 = 0.5801$

b) $\mu_x = np = 10 * 0.768 = 7.68$,
$\sigma_x = \sqrt{npq} = \sqrt{10 * 0.768 * 0.232} \approx 1.3348$

c) $z = \dfrac{10 - 7.68}{1.3348} \approx 1.738 \Rightarrow$ not really.
Winning with the Aces all ten times would still be less than 2 standard deviations above the expected number of wins.

d) $\mu_x - 2\sigma_x \approx 5.01$ and $\mu_x + 2\sigma_x \approx 10.35 \Rightarrow$ Anywhere from 6 to 10 wins.

e) $n = 100$, $p = 0.768$, $q = 0.232$,
$\mu_x = np = 100 * 0.768 = 76.8$,
$\sigma_x = \sqrt{npq} = \sqrt{100 * 0.768 * 0.232} \approx 4.2211$

f) $z = \dfrac{100 - 76.8}{4.2211} \approx 5.496 \Rightarrow$ Yes, in fact, winning all 100 hands would be very unusual, because this is more than 3 standard deviations above the mean.

g) $\mu_x - 2\sigma_x \approx 68.36$ and
$\mu_x + 2\sigma_x \approx 85.24 \Rightarrow$ Anywhere from 69 to 85 wins are expected.

Chapter Problem:

1) a) We know the value of 7 of the cards. 45 cards remain unseen and possible. We have seen three Kings, so only 1 remains. We have seen one 8 and one 2, so 3 of each of those remain. Therefore,

$P(K \text{ or } 8 \text{ or } 2) = \dfrac{1 + 3 + 3}{45} \approx 0.1556$

b) This is a bit tricky to get right. Let me show you a common mistake as a start and we will fix it from there. We don't want the board to pair on the turn. We saw above that there are 7 cards that can make that happen. We will subtract these away from the 45 remaining unseen cards. We then want the river card to pair one of the community cards. We must remember that the river card might pair the turn card as well as the King, 8, or 2. For example, if the turn is a 5, then if any of the three remaining 5's comes on the river, we will win. Here is the math:

$P(NoPair_{turn} \, \& \, Pair_{river}) =$
$\dfrac{45 - 7}{45} * \dfrac{1 + 3 + 3 + 3}{44} \approx 0.1919$

As complicated as this answer is to get, it still contains a small error. If the turn card is an Ace or a Jack, then only two of those cards remain on the river. We need to consider this when doing the math.

$P\Big(\big((A \text{ or } J)_{turn} \, \& \, (PairedBoard)_{river}\big) \text{ or }$
$\big((not(A \text{ or } J) \, \& \, NoPair)_{turn} \, \& \, (PairedBoard)_{river}\big)\Big)$
$= \dfrac{6}{45} * \dfrac{1 + 3 + 3 + 2}{44} + \dfrac{45 - 7 - 6}{45} * \dfrac{1 + 3 + 3 + 3}{44}$
≈ 0.1889

c) For this part, we simply add the answers from parts (a) and (b).

$$\frac{7}{45} + \frac{6}{45} * \frac{9}{44} + \frac{32}{45} * \frac{10}{44} \approx 0.3444$$

2) a) Using the answer of 0.34444 from part (c).

	x	$P(x)$	$x \cdot P(x)$
call & win	1060	0.3444	365.064
call & lose	-370	0.6556	-242.572
		1.0000	122.492

b) $\mu_x = 122.492$, in the long run, we would show an average profit of $122.492 for each time we make this call in this situation.

c) Yes, in the long run, such calls will be profitable. The outcome of this particular hand is uncertain. Cross your fingers and call.

3) $n = 10$, $p = 0.3444$, $q = 1 - p = 0.6556$

a) $\mu_y = np = 10 * 0.3444 = 3.444$,

$\sigma_y = \sqrt{npq} = \sqrt{10 * 0.3444 * 0.6556} \approx 1.5026$

b) $\mu_y - 2\sigma_y \approx 0.4388$ and

$\mu_y + 2\sigma_y \approx 6.4492 \Rightarrow$ Anywhere from 1 to 6 wins are expected.

c) Since we will play ten such hands, if we only win 1 such hand, then we will lose 9 such hands. In the hand we win, we would win $1060. In the 9 we lose, we would lose $370 nine times. So, this is represented by $-9 * \$370 = -\$3330$. So, when the ten hands are completed this way, our result is given by: $\$1060 - 9 * \$370 = -\$2270$.

d) If we win 6 of the ten hands, then we will lose 4. So our overall result for the ten hands would be represented by: $6 * \$1060 - 4 * \$370 = \$4880$.

Note: After ten plays of making the correct mathematical decision, we might still lose $2270, but the upside is a possible profit of $4880.

Section 6.1:

1) Normal distributions are bell - shaped.

2) If a population is normally distributed, then the area under the corresponding normal curve can be used to approximate population relative frequencies.

3) If a random variable is normally distributed, then the area under the corresponding normal curve can be used to approximate probabilities for the random variable.

4) 4 properties of normal curves.
   a) Total area under the curve is 1.
   b) Curve is symmetric about its mean.
   c) Curve extends indefinitely in both directions and the height approaches zero on each side.
   d) Almost all of the area lies between $\mu - 3\sigma$ and $\mu + 3\sigma$.

5) If σ becomes larger, then the normal curve becomes shorter and wider. If σ becomes smaller, then the normal curve becomes taller and narrower.

6) The normal distribution that has a mean, $\mu = 0$, and standard deviation, $\sigma = 1$, is called the standard normal distribution.

7) The units on the standard normal curve represent the number of standard deviations away from the mean.

9) a) This curve will be bell-shaped, centered at $\mu = 10$, and flatten out at $\mu - 3\sigma = 10 - 3 * 2 = 4$ and $\mu + 3\sigma = 10 + 3 * 2 = 16$.

   b) This curve will also be bell-shaped, but it will be centered at $\mu = 12$, and will flatten out at $\mu - 3\sigma = 12 - 3 * 3 = 3$ and $\mu + 3\sigma = 12 + 3 * 3 = 21$. Because this curve is wider, it will be shorter to maintain the constant area of 1.

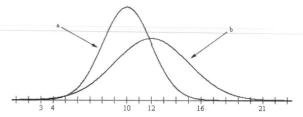

11) a) This curve will be centered at $\mu = 24.1$, and will flatten out at
$\mu - 3\sigma = 24.1 - 3*2.307 = 17.179$ and
$\mu + 3\sigma = 24.1 + 3*2.307 = 31.021$.

b) $z = \dfrac{30 - 24.1}{2.307} \approx 2.557$; Such a snake would be 2.557 standard deviations above the mean.

c) We need the area between 20 and 30.

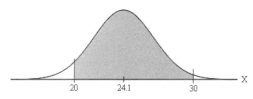

d) This time, we want to shade the area that lies between the z-scores for the x-values from part (c). $z = \dfrac{20 - 24.1}{2.307} \approx -1.777$

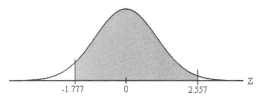

13) a) This curve will be centered at $\mu = 115$, and will flatten out at
$\mu - 3\sigma = 115 - 3*7.062 = 93.814$ and
$\mu + 3\sigma = 115 + 3*7.062 = 136.186$.

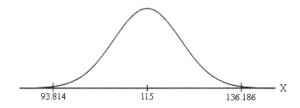

b) $z = \dfrac{134 - 115}{7.062} \approx 2.690 \Rightarrow$ the temperature that day was 2.690 standard deviations above the mean.

c) We need all the area to the right of 110.

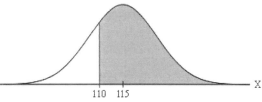

d) This time, we want the area to the right of the z-score for 110.
$z = \dfrac{110 - 115}{7.062} \approx -0.708$

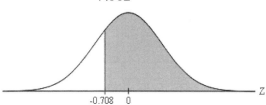

Section 6.2:

15) When using the normalcdf command, we must enter both the <u>left</u> - hand <u>boundary</u> and the <u>right</u> - hand <u>boundary</u> of the region.

16) When using the invNorm command, we only need to enter the area on the <u>left</u> of the boundary we are seeking.

17) z_α tells us that there is an area of α to the <u>right</u> of the z we are looking for.

18) If we are using the normalcdf command and we need to enter a lower boundary of $-\infty$, then we enter -1×10^{99} <u>or -I</u> in the calculator. If we need to enter ∞, then we will use 1×10^{99} <u>or I</u>.

19) a) The area appears to be more than half.

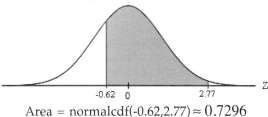

Area = normalcdf(-0.62,2.77) ≈ 0.7296

b)   This appears to be most of the area under
     the curve.

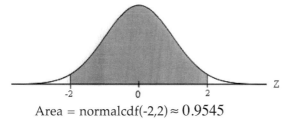

Area = normalcdf(-2,2) ≈ 0.9545

c)   Use $-1 \times 10^{99} = -I$ for the lower boundary.
     The area appears close to 1.

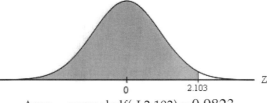

Area = normalcdf(-I,2.103) ≈ 0.9823

d)   Use $1 \times 10^{99} = I$ as the upper boundary.
     The area appears to be small.

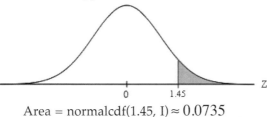

Area = normalcdf(1.45, I) ≈ 0.0735

21) a)   Almost all the area appears to be shaded.

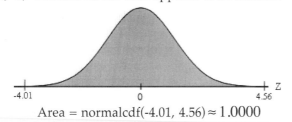

Area = normalcdf(-4.01, 4.56) ≈ 1.0000

b)   Almost no area is shaded this time. We
     will use $-1 \times 10^{99} = -I$ for the lower
     boundary.

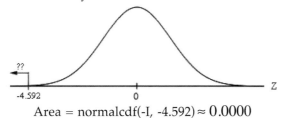

Area = normalcdf(-I, -4.592) ≈ 0.0000

c)   Again, almost no area appears to be
     shaded. We will use $1 \times 10^{99} = I$ for the
     upper boundary.

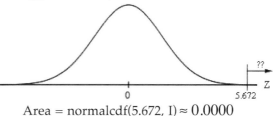

Area = normalcdf(5.672, I) ≈ 0.0000

23) All probabilities will be found using the
     corresponding area under the standard normal
     curve.

a)   It appears that far less than half of the
     area is shaded.

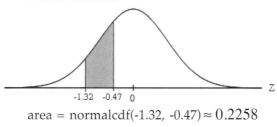

area = normalcdf(-1.32, -0.47) ≈ 0.2258

b)   Only a small amount of area is shaded. We
     will use $-1 \times 10^{99} = -I$ for the lower
     boundary.

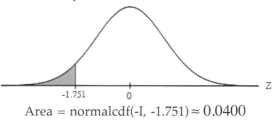

Area = normalcdf(-I, -1.751) ≈ 0.0400

c)   Most of the area is shaded. We will use
     $1 \times 10^{99} = I$ for the upper boundary.

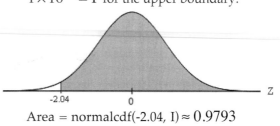

Area = normalcdf(-2.04, I) ≈ 0.9793

25) All probabilities will be found using the corresponding area under the standard normal curve.

a) We could find the two shaded area and add, or we could find the unwanted area and subtract from 1.

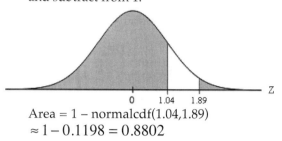

Area = 1 – normalcdf(1.04,1.89)
$\approx 1 - 0.1198 = 0.8802$

b) For an AND question, we want the overlap of the two parts. We see in the graph below that the overlap is from 1 to 2.

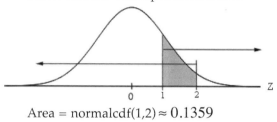

Area = normalcdf(1,2) ≈ 0.1359

27) Problems that give area and ask for z-scores are working backwards questions and require the use of the invNorm function.
Recall: we must enter the area to the left when using this function.

a) The area to the left is small, so the z-score we need will be on the left side of the graph. Since we are given an area to the left, we can go straight to the invNorm function.

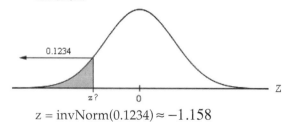

z = invNorm(0.1234) ≈ -1.158

b) The area to the left is large, so the z-score will be on the right side of the graph.

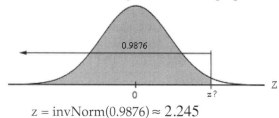

z = invNorm(0.9876) ≈ 2.245

c) The area to the right is small, so the z will be on the right. Since we are given an area to the right, we must subtract from 1 to get the area on the left.

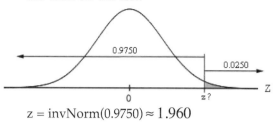

z = invNorm(0.9750) ≈ 1.960

d) If the area in the middle is 0.90. Then subtracting from 1, we have 0.10 remaining. We divide that equally among the two sides, so we have 0.05 on each side.

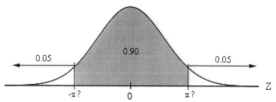

Since we must enter an area on the left, it is easiest to find the negative z first. Then, by symmetry, the other z will be the same, but positive.

-z = invNorm(0.05) $\approx -1.645 \Rightarrow z \approx 1.645$

29) a) $z_{0.01}$ is the z-score with an area of 0.01 to its right. Since, this is a small amount of area to the right, the z is on the right. We subtract from 1 to find the area 0.99 on the left.

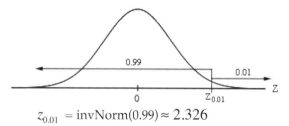

$z_{0.01}$ = invNorm(0.99) ≈ 2.326

b) $z_{0.05}$ is the z-score with an area of 0.05 to its right. Since, this is a small amount of area to the right, the z is on the right. We subtract from 1 to find the area 0.95 on the left.

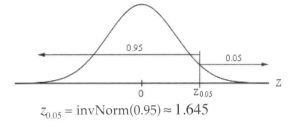

$z_{0.05}$ = invNorm(0.95) ≈ 1.645

c) $z_{0.80}$ is the z-score with an area of 0.80 to its right. Since, this is a large amount of area to the right, the z is on the left. We subtract from 1 to find the area 0.20 on the left.

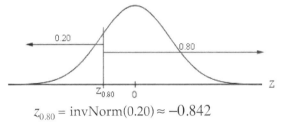

$z_{0.80}$ = invNorm(0.20) ≈ −0.842

Section 6.3:

31) We convert areas under normal curves to area under the standard normal curve by calculating the <u>z-scores</u> for the x-value boundaries of the region of interest.

32) The empirical rule for <u>normal</u> distributions states that 68.27% of the data lies within <u>1</u> standard deviation of the mean, <u>95.45</u> % lies within 2 standard deviations of the mean, and <u>99.73</u> % lies within 3 standard deviations of the mean.

33) If an x-value has a z-score of 1.57, then that x-value is 1.57 <u>standard</u> <u>deviations</u> <u>above</u> the <u>mean</u> .

34) The 74th percentile, or P_{74}, is the x-value that has an area of <u>0.74</u> to its <u>left</u> .

35) a)   We are given x-values, so we need to find z-scores for each of them.

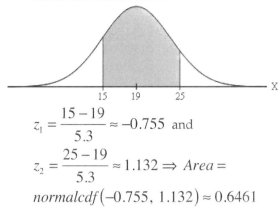

$z_1 = \dfrac{15 - 19}{5.3} ≈ -0.755$ and

$z_2 = \dfrac{25 - 19}{5.3} ≈ 1.132 \Rightarrow Area =$

$normalcdf(-0.755, 1.132) ≈ 0.6461$

b)   We begin by finding the z-score for 20. We will use $1 \times 10^{99} = I$ for the upper boundary.

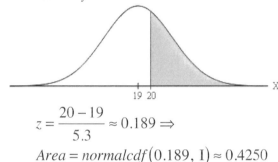

$z = \dfrac{20 - 19}{5.3} ≈ 0.189 \Rightarrow$

$Area = normalcdf(0.189, I) ≈ 0.4250$

c)   We will find the z-score for 10 and use $-1 \times 10^{99} = -I$ for the lower boundary.

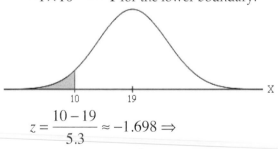

$z = \dfrac{10 - 19}{5.3} ≈ -1.698 \Rightarrow$

$Area = normalcdf(-I, -1.698) ≈ 0.0448$

37) a) The area to the right is small, so the x will be on the right. Sine the area to the right is given, we subtract from 1 to find the area of 0.90 to the left. Since we are working backwards here, we will use invNorm.

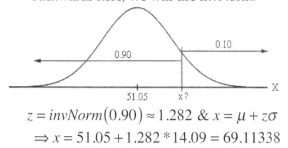

$$z = invNorm(0.90) \approx 1.282 \;\&\; x = \mu + z\sigma$$
$$\Rightarrow x = 51.05 + 1.282 * 14.09 = 69.11338$$

b) The area to the left is large, so the x will be on the right. We now use invNorm to find the z, and then we convert to an x-value.

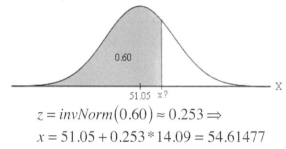

$$z = invNorm(0.60) \approx 0.253 \Rightarrow$$
$$x = 51.05 + 0.253 * 14.09 = 54.61477$$

c) If the middle area is 0.90, then we split the remaining 0.10 to get 0.05 on each side. Because of symmetry, the z on the left and the z on the right will be opposites of each other. Since we have the area to the left of –z on our graph, we will find it first.

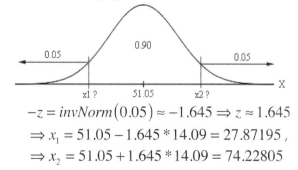

$$-z = invNorm(0.05) \approx -1.645 \Rightarrow z \approx 1.645$$
$$\Rightarrow x_1 = 51.05 - 1.645 * 14.09 = 27.87195 ,$$
$$\Rightarrow x_2 = 51.05 + 1.645 * 14.09 = 74.22805$$

39) a) The area to the right of 50 will equal the probability we are looking for. We will use $1 \times 10^{99} = I$ for our upper boundary.

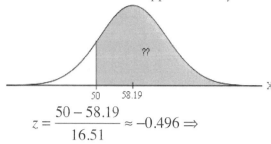

$$z = \frac{50 - 58.19}{16.51} \approx -0.496 \Rightarrow$$
$$Area = normalcdf(-0.496,\, I) \approx 0.6901$$

b) We need to find the two shaded areas and add them up, or we could just find the unshaded area and subtract that from one. Either way, we need to find the z-scores first.

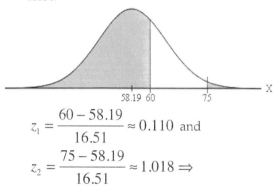

$$z_1 = \frac{60 - 58.19}{16.51} \approx 0.110 \text{ and}$$
$$z_2 = \frac{75 - 58.19}{16.51} \approx 1.018 \Rightarrow$$
$$Total\ Shaded\ Area =$$
$$1 - normalcdf(0.110,\, 1.018) \approx 0.6981$$

c) The quartiles divide the area under a normal curve into 4 equal parts. That means the area in each part will be 0.25. See the sketch below.

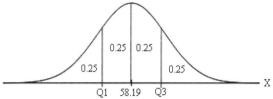

Since have of the area is to the left of the mean and half of the area is to the right, the mean is also the median. To find Q_1 and Q_3, we must first find their z-scores and then convert them to x-values. Because of symmetry, they will have equal but opposite z-scores.

$-z = invNorm(0.25) \approx -0.674 \Rightarrow z \approx 0.674$

$Q_1 = 58.19 - 0.674 * 16.51 \approx 47.06$

$Q_2 = M = \mu = 58.19$

$Q_3 = 58.19 + 0.674 * 16.51 \approx 69.32$

41) $\mu = 42.56$ and $\sigma = 1.573$

a) The decimal form of the percentage will equal the area between 40 and 45.

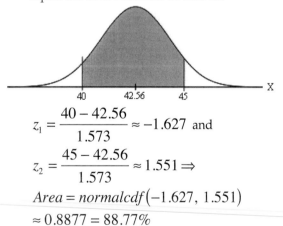

$z_1 = \dfrac{40 - 42.56}{1.573} \approx -1.627$ and

$z_2 = \dfrac{45 - 42.56}{1.573} \approx 1.551 \Rightarrow$

$Area = normalcdf(-1.627, 1.551)$

$\approx 0.8877 = 88.77\%$

b) At least indicates 42 or higher. We will use $1 \times 10^{99} = I$ for our upper boundary.

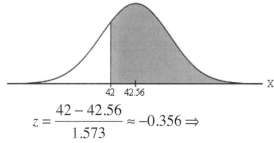

$z = \dfrac{42 - 42.56}{1.573} \approx -0.356 \Rightarrow$

$Area = normalcdf(-0.356, I) \approx 0.6391 = 63.91\%$

c) The tenth percentile will have an area of 0.10 to its left. Since we know the area and are looking for the boundary, we use invNorm.

$z = invNorm(0.10) \approx -1.282 \Rightarrow$

$P_{10} = x = 42.56 - 1.282 * 1.573 \approx 40.54$

10% of 5-yr old girls have heights below 40.54 inches tall.

d) For a normal curve, the areas under the graph and the z-scores are always the same when finding quartiles.

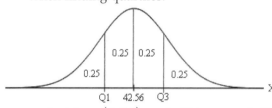

$-z = invNorm(0.25) \approx -0.674 \Rightarrow z \approx 0.674$

$Q_1 = 42.56 - 0.674 * 1.573 \approx 41.50$

$Q_2 = M = \mu = 42.56$

$Q_3 = 42.56 + 0.674 * 1.573 \approx 43.62$

43) $\mu = 24.1$ and $\sigma = 2.307$

a) The area to the right of 30 will be the decimal form of the percentage we need. We will use $1 \times 10^{99} = I$ for our upper boundary.

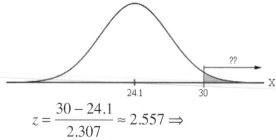

$z = \dfrac{30 - 24.1}{2.307} \approx 2.557 \Rightarrow$

$Area = normalcdf(2.557, I) \approx 0.0053 = 0.53\%$

b) Again we will find the area and then convert to a percentage.

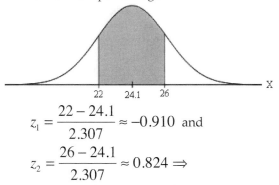

$$z_1 = \frac{22 - 24.1}{2.307} \approx -0.910 \text{ and}$$

$$z_2 = \frac{26 - 24.1}{2.307} \approx 0.824 \Rightarrow$$

$Area = normalcdf(-0.910, 0.824) \approx 0.6136 = 61.36\%$

c) To be in the longest 1% of these snakes, you would have to be a big snake. So the 1% or area of 0.01 will be on the right. invNorm works with areas to the left, so we subtract from 1 to get 0.99

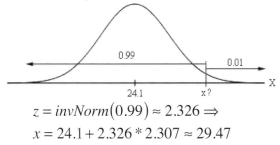

$z = invNorm(0.99) \approx 2.326 \Rightarrow$

$x = 24.1 + 2.326 * 2.307 \approx 29.47$

The snake would have to be at least 29.47 feet long to be in the longest 1%.

d) For a normal curve, the areas under the graph and the z-scores are always the same when finding quartiles.

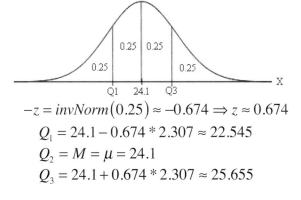

$-z = invNorm(0.25) \approx -0.674 \Rightarrow z \approx 0.674$

$Q_1 = 24.1 - 0.674 * 2.307 \approx 22.545$

$Q_2 = M = \mu = 24.1$

$Q_3 = 24.1 + 0.674 * 2.307 \approx 25.655$

45) All probabilities will be found by using the corresponding area under the normal curve.

a) We need the area to the right of 100. We will use $1 \times 10^{99} = I$ for our upper boundary.

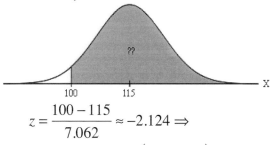

$$z = \frac{100 - 115}{7.062} \approx -2.124 \Rightarrow$$

$Area = normalcdf(-2.124, I) \approx 0.9832$

b) This time we need the area between 95 and 105.

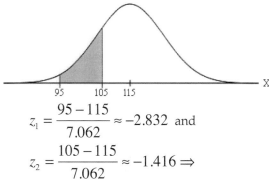

$$z_1 = \frac{95 - 115}{7.062} \approx -2.832 \text{ and}$$

$$z_2 = \frac{105 - 115}{7.062} \approx -1.416 \Rightarrow$$

$Area = normalcdf(-2.832, -1.416) \approx 0.0761$

c) The 20th percentile will have an area of 0.20 to its left.

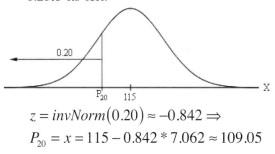

$z = invNorm(0.20) \approx -0.842 \Rightarrow$

$P_{20} = x = 115 - 0.842 * 7.062 \approx 109.05$

20% of the days in July have a high temperature below 109.05°F.

d) We will need to use the conditional probability rule for this one.

$$P(X \leq 120 | X > 100) =$$

$$\frac{P(X \leq 120 \ \& \ X > 100)}{P(X > 100)} = \frac{P(100 < X \leq 120)}{P(X > 100)}$$

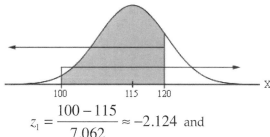

$$z_1 = \frac{100 - 115}{7.062} \approx -2.124 \ \text{and}$$

$$z_2 = \frac{120 - 115}{7.062} \approx 0.708 \Rightarrow$$

$$P(100 < X \leq 120) =$$

$$normalcdf(-2.124, \ 0.708) \approx 0.7437$$

$$P(X > 100) =$$

$$normalcdf(-2.124, \ I) \approx 0.9832 \Rightarrow$$

$$P(X \leq 120 | X > 100) \approx \frac{0.7437}{0.9832} \approx 0.7564$$

47) a) Since X is counting the number of successes in 40 trials this is a binomial distribution. We also need to find n, p, and q. The value of n = 40 because there are 40 trials. p is the probability of a success and it is not given, but we can figure it out.

$$p = P(\text{success in a single trial}) = P(temp < 98)$$

The problem tells us that temperature is normally distributed with $\mu_{temp} = 98.2$ and $\sigma_{temp} = 0.352$. So we can find p using area under this curve. We will use $-1 \times 10^{99} = -I$ for the lower boundary.

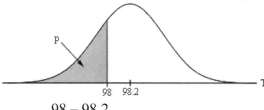

$$z = \frac{98 - 98.2}{0.352} \approx -0.568 \Rightarrow$$

$$p = normalcdf(-I, \ -0.568) \approx 0.2850$$

X has the binomial distribution with n = 40, p = 0.2850, and q = 1 − p = 0.7150.

b) We should use a z-score to answer this question, but we need to be careful about the details. They are asking if it would be unusual if the number of successes is zero. So, we have to use the mean and standard deviation for X, not for temperature when computing this z-score. First we must find these values.

$$\mu_X = np = 40 * 0.2850 = 11.4$$

$$\sigma_X = \sqrt{npq} = \sqrt{40 * 0.285 * 0.715} \approx 2.8550$$

$$z = \frac{0 - 11.4}{2.8550} \approx -3.993 \Rightarrow$$

Yes, $z \approx -3.993 \Rightarrow$ in fact, zero successes is considered very unusual because it is more than 3 standard deviations below the mean.

49) Recall: $\mu = 42.56$ and $\sigma = 1.573$.

a) We should recognize 68.27% from the Empirical Rule as the percentage of data that lies within 1 standard deviation of the mean for normal data sets. $\mu - \sigma = 40.987$ and $\mu + \sigma = 44.133$. So we fill in the blanks with 40.987 and 44.133 in.

b) This time the Empirical Rule tells us to use 2 standard deviations. $\mu - 2\sigma = 39.414$ and $\mu + 2\sigma = 45.706$. So we fill in the blanks with 39.414 and 45.706 in.

c) This time we use 3 standard deviations. $\mu - 3\sigma = 37.841$ and $\mu + 3\sigma = 47.279$. So we fill in the blanks with 37.841 and 47.279 in.

d) 90% is not from the Empirical Rule. So, we must figure out how many standard deviations away from the mean we need by finding the 2 z-scores that trap an area of 0.90 in the middle with equal outside areas.

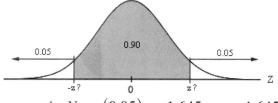

$$-z = invNorm(0.05) \approx -1.645 \Rightarrow z \approx 1.645$$

$$\mu - 1.645\sigma \approx 39.972 \ \text{and}$$

$$\mu + 1.645\sigma \approx 45.148. \ \text{So, we fill in the}$$
blanks with 39.972 and 45.148 in.

Section 6.4:

51) We approximate binomial probabilities using the area of the <u>histogram</u> bars. To do this accurately, we must use <u>1/2</u> marks as the boundaries of the region we find the area of.

52) If $np \geq \underline{5}$ and $nq \geq \underline{5}$, then a binomial distribution is considered to be approximately <u>normal</u>.

53) a) $\begin{array}{l} np = 340(0.894) = 303.96 \geq 5 \\ nq = 340(0.106) = 36.04 \geq 5 \end{array} \Rightarrow$ This binomial distribution is approx. normal and the requirements have been met.

b) We begin by finding the mean and standard deviation for this binomial variable.

$\mu_x = np = 340 * 0.894 = 303.96$

$\sigma_x = \sqrt{npq} = \sqrt{340 * 0.894 * 0.106} \approx 5.6762$

To find $P(X = 300)$, we need to approximate the area of the bar for 300.

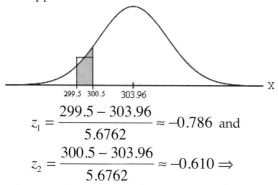

$z_1 = \dfrac{299.5 - 303.96}{5.6762} \approx -0.786$ and

$z_2 = \dfrac{300.5 - 303.96}{5.6762} \approx -0.610 \Rightarrow$

$P(X = 300) \approx normalcdf(-0.786, -0.610) \approx 0.0550$

c) For this one we want to start at the left hand side of the bar for 300 and end at the left hand side of the bar for 310 (since 310 is not included.)

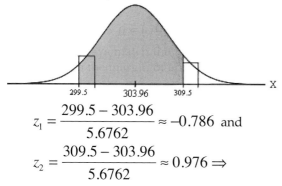

$z_1 = \dfrac{299.5 - 303.96}{5.6762} \approx -0.786$ and

$z_2 = \dfrac{309.5 - 303.96}{5.6762} \approx 0.976 \Rightarrow$

$P(300 \leq X < 310) \approx$
$normalcdf(-0.786, 0.976) \approx 0.6195$

d) To approximate $P(X > 290)$, we want to use the right side of the bar for 290 (since it is not included) as our lower boundary and $1 \times 10^{99} = I$ as our upper boundary.

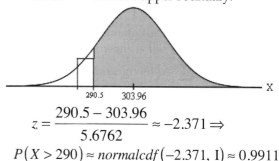

$z = \dfrac{290.5 - 303.96}{5.6762} \approx -2.371 \Rightarrow$

$P(X > 290) \approx normalcdf(-2.371, I) \approx 0.9911$

55) This is a binomial distribution with $n = 1329$, $p = 0.607$, and $q = 1 - p = 0.393$. Since we will be using the normal approximation, we need to find the mean and standard deviation.

$\mu_x = np = 806.703$, $\sigma_x = \sqrt{npq} \approx 17.805$

a) To approximate this probability, we need to approximate the area of the histogram bar for 800 using the area under the corresponding normal curve.

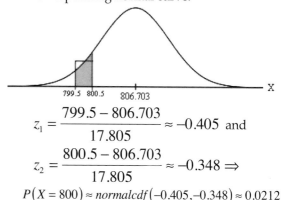

$z_1 = \dfrac{799.5 - 806.703}{17.805} \approx -0.405$ and

$z_2 = \dfrac{800.5 - 806.703}{17.805} \approx -0.348 \Rightarrow$

$P(X = 800) \approx normalcdf(-0.405, -0.348) \approx 0.0212$

b) At least 750 includes the 750, so this time we want to find $P(X \geq 750)$. We will use 749.5 as our lower boundary (to include the 750) and we will use $1 \times 10^{99} = I$ as our upper boundary.

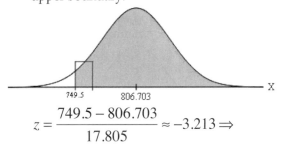

$$z = \frac{749.5 - 806.703}{17.805} \approx -3.213 \Rightarrow$$

$$P(X \geq 750) \approx normalcdf(-3.213, I) \approx 0.9993$$

57) This is a binomial distribution with $n = 100$, $p = 0.768$, and $q = 1 - p = 0.232$.

a) $\begin{array}{l} np = 76.8 \geq 5 \\ nq = 23.2 \geq 5 \end{array} \Rightarrow$ This binomial distribution is approx. normal, so the requirements have been met.

b) Before we can use the normal approximation, we must determine the mean and standard deviation.

$\mu_X = np = 76.8$ and

$\sigma_X = \sqrt{npq} \approx 4.2211$.

To find $P(X < 80)$, we will use $-1 \times 10^{99} = -I$ as our lower boundary and 79.5 as our upper boundary (since 80 is not included.)

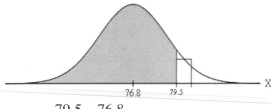

$$z = \frac{79.5 - 76.8}{4.2211} \approx 0.640 \Rightarrow$$

$$P(X < 80) = normalcdf(-I, 0.640) \approx 0.7389$$

c) To find $P(X \geq 90)$, we will use 89.5 as our lower boundary (since 90 is included) and we will use $1 \times 10^{99} = I$ as our upper boundary.

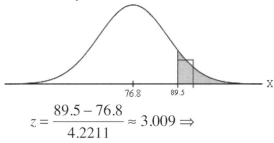

$$z = \frac{89.5 - 76.8}{4.2211} \approx 3.009 \Rightarrow$$

$$P(X \geq 90) \approx normalcdf(3.009, I) \approx 0.0013$$

d) $\mu_X - 2\sigma_X \approx 68.4$ and $\mu_X + 2\sigma_X \approx 85.5$, so we expect the two aces to win anywhere from 68 to 85 of the 100 times.

59) a) Because X is a count of the number of successes in 200 trials, this is a binomial distribution. The n is 200, but we need to figure out the value of p from the information provided.

$p = P(\text{success}) = P(Battery > 12)$.

The problem tells us that the battery life, B, is normally distributed with $\mu_B = 11.74$ and $\sigma_B = 0.7833$. Our lower boundary is 12 and we will use $1 \times 10^{99} = I$ for the upper boundary.

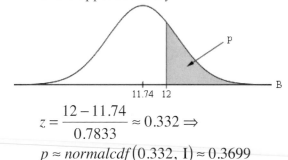

$$z = \frac{12 - 11.74}{0.7833} \approx 0.332 \Rightarrow$$

$$p \approx normalcdf(0.332, I) \approx 0.3699$$

X has the binomial distribution with $n = 200$, $p = 0.3699$, and $q = 1 - p = 0.6301$.

b) The key to this part is to realize we are being asked a probability question about X, therefore we can't use the mean and standard deviation that were given. Those were for battery life, B. We need to calculate the mean and standard deviation for X using n, p, and q.

$$\mu_X = np = 200 * 0.3699 = 73.98 \text{ and}$$
$$\sigma_X = \sqrt{npq} = \sqrt{200 * 0.3699 * 0.6301} \approx 6.8275$$

Now, finding $P(X > 100)$ will be done using a normal approximation. We will use 100.5 as our lower boundary (since 100 is not included), and we will use $1 \times 10^{99} = I$ as our upper boundary.

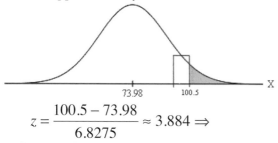

$$z = \frac{100.5 - 73.98}{6.8275} \approx 3.884 \Rightarrow$$
$$P(X > 100) \approx normalcdf(3.884, I) \approx 0.0001$$

Chapter Problem:

a) The histogram is roughly bell-shaped. Therefore, I would conclude that there is a reasonable possibility that the sample was taken from a normal population.
b) The p-value is greater than 0.05. Therefore, I would conclude that there is a reasonable possibility that the sample was taken from a normal population.
c) The subcommand used for the random command specified a normal population. Since the population really is normal, the samples lead to the correct conclusion in both part (a) and (b).

Section 7.1:

1) A point estimate is a single value calculated from a <u>sample</u> and used to estimate a population quantity.

2) Sampling error is the error that results from using an estimate obtained from a <u>sample</u> rather than a <u>census</u> to estimate a population quantity.

3) a) $\mu = \dfrac{\sum x}{4} = 100.5$

bc)

Sample	$\bar{x}$
84, 92	88
84, 105	94.5
84, 121	102.5
92, 105	98.5
92, 121	106.5
105, 121	113

d) $P(\bar{x} = \mu) = P(\bar{x} = 100.5) = \dfrac{0}{6} = 0\%$

e) $P(100.5 - 3 \le \bar{x} \le 100.5 + 3) =$
    $P(97.5 \le \bar{x} \le 103.5) = \dfrac{2}{6} \approx 33.33\%$

f) $P(100.5 - 6 \le \bar{x} \le 100.5 + 6) =$
    $P(94.5 \le \bar{x} \le 106.5) = \dfrac{4}{6} \approx 66.67\%$

5) a) $\mu = \dfrac{\sum x}{6} \approx 19.33$

bc)

Sample	$\bar{x}$
12, 16, 19, 20, 22	17.8
12, 16, 19, 20, 27	18.8
12, 16, 19, 22, 27	19.2
12, 16, 20, 22, 27	19.4
12, 19, 20, 22, 27	20
16, 19, 20, 22, 27	20.8

d) $P(\bar{x} = \mu) = P(\bar{x} = 19.33) = \dfrac{0}{6} = 0\%$

e) $P(19.33 - 1 \le \bar{x} \le 19.33 + 1) =$
    $P(18.33 \le \bar{x} \le 20.33) = \dfrac{4}{6} \approx 66.67\%$

f) $P(19.33 - 2 \le \bar{x} \le 19.33 + 2) =$
    $P(17.33 \le \bar{x} \le 21.33) = \dfrac{6}{6} = 100\%$

7) Increasing the amount of error we considered to be acceptable increased our chance of getting an acceptable estimate.

9) a) $\mu = \dfrac{\sum x}{4} = 100.5$

bc)

Sample	$\bar{x}$
84, 92, 105	93.67
84, 92, 121	99
84, 105, 121	103.33
92, 105, 121	106

d) $P(\bar{x} = \mu) = P(\bar{x} = 100.5) = \dfrac{0}{4} = 0\%$

e) $P(100.5 - 3 \le \bar{x} \le 100.5 + 3) =$

$P(97.5 \le \bar{x} \le 103.5) = \dfrac{2}{4} = 50\%$

f) $P(100.5 - 6 \le \bar{x} \le 100.5 + 6) =$

$P(94.5 \le \bar{x} \le 106.5) = \dfrac{3}{4} = 75\%$

The $P(\bar{x} = \mu)$ did not improve.
$P(\mu - 3 \le \bar{x} \le \mu + 3)$ increased from 33.33% to 50%. $P(\mu - 6 \le \bar{x} \le \mu + 6)$ increased from 66.67% to 75%. So, if we are willing to accept some sampling error, it appears that increasing the sample size increases our chance of getting an acceptable estimate.

11) There is usually a very bad chance of no sampling error. Recall: $P(\bar{x} = \mu) \approx 0$

Section 7.2:

13) $\mu_{\bar{x}} = \mu$ tells us that $\bar{x}$ is a random variable and that if you average all possible values of the <u>sample</u> mean, then the result equals the <u>population</u> mean.

14) $\sigma_{\bar{x}} \approx \dfrac{\sigma}{\sqrt{n}}$ is good news because it tells us that the higher the sample size the closer the possible values of $\bar{x}$ get to the <u>population mean</u>.

15) a) Enter the data into L1 and then choose STAT > CALC > 1-Var Stats L1
$\mu = 100.5$; $\sigma \approx 14.009$

bcd)

Sample	$\bar{x}$	$P(\bar{x})$	$\bar{x} \cdot P(\bar{x})$	$(\bar{x} - \mu_{\bar{x}})^2 P(\bar{x})$
84, 92	88	1/6	14.667	26.0417
84, 105	94.5	1/6	15.75	6
84, 121	102.5	1/6	17.083	0.6667
92, 105	98.5	1/6	16.417	0.6667
92, 121	106.5	1/6	17.75	6
105, 121	113	1/6	18.833	26.0417
			100.5	65.4168

$\mu_{\bar{x}} = \sum \bar{x} \cdot P(\bar{x}) = 100.5$;

$\sigma_{\bar{x}} = \sqrt{(\bar{x} - \mu_{\bar{x}})^2 P(\bar{x})} = \sqrt{65.4168} \approx 8.0881$

e) $\sigma_{\bar{x}} = \dfrac{14.009}{\sqrt{2}} \sqrt{\dfrac{4-2}{4-1}} \approx 8.0881$

17) We are given that $\mu = 112$ and $\sigma = 38.2$.

a) $\mu_{\bar{x}} = \mu = 112$; $\sigma_{\bar{x}} \approx \dfrac{38.2}{\sqrt{10}} \approx 12.080$

b) $\mu_{\bar{x}} = \mu = 112$; $\sigma_{\bar{x}} \approx \dfrac{38.2}{\sqrt{30}} \approx 6.9743$

c) None

d) It decreased it. This happens because we are dividing by the square root of the sample size. Larger n, means larger denominator, means small answer.

19) We are given that $\mu = 5.6$ and $\sigma = 1.31$.

a) I expect the error to be less than 2σ.
$2\sigma = 2 * 1.31 = 2.62 \Rightarrow$ The expected error is less than 2.62 lbs.

b) $\mu_{\bar{x}} = \mu = 5.6$ and $\sigma_{\bar{x}} \approx \dfrac{1.31}{\sqrt{8}} \approx 0.46315$

c) Expected error is less than $2\sigma_{\bar{x}}$.
$2\sigma_{\bar{x}} \approx 2 * 0.46315 = 0.92630 \Rightarrow$ The expected error is less than 0.92630 lbs.

d) Not necessarily. For example, an error of 0.85 lbs would be more than 0.75 lbs yet not unusual because it is smaller than the expected error.

e) $\mu_{\bar{x}} = \mu = 5.6$ and $\sigma_{\bar{x}} \approx \dfrac{1.31}{\sqrt{25}} = 0.262$

f) Less than $2\sigma_{\bar{x}} \approx 0.524$ lbs.

g) Yes, because $2\sigma_{\bar{x}} \approx 0.524$, that would be an $\bar{x}$ more than 2 standard deviations away from its mean.

21) $2\sigma_{\bar{x}} < 0.25 \Rightarrow 2\dfrac{1.31}{\sqrt{n}} < 0.25 \Rightarrow$

$2.62 < 0.25\sqrt{n} \Rightarrow \dfrac{2.62}{0.25} < \sqrt{n} \Rightarrow$

$n > \left(\dfrac{2.62}{0.25}\right)^2 \approx 109.8304$. So we need 110 or more puppies.

Section 7.3:

23) If our sample is taken from a normal population, then $\bar{x}$ will also be normally distributed, regardless of the sample size.

24) If our sample size is greater than or equal to 30, then $\bar{x}$ will be normally distributed regardless of the distribution of the original population. This is the statement of the Central Limit Theorem.

25) If the sample size is $15 \leq n < 30$, and if the population is not severely skewed, then $\bar{x}$ will be normal.

26) False. A large sample ensures that $\bar{x}$ (not the population) will be normally distributed.

27) a) $P(x > 150)$ is unknown since we don't know the distribution of the population. The distribution of x and the population are always the same.

b) Since n = 85 ≥ 30, the possible values of $\bar{x}$ are normal with $\mu_{\bar{x}} = \mu = 153.7$ and

$\sigma_{\bar{x}} \approx \dfrac{16.973}{\sqrt{85}} \approx 1.8410$

c) We need to find the area to the right of $\bar{x} = 150$ under the normal curve described in part (b).

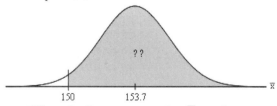

When finding a z-score for $\bar{x}$, make sure that you use $\mu_{\bar{x}}$ and $\sigma_{\bar{x}}$.

$z = \dfrac{\bar{x} - \mu_{\bar{x}}}{\sigma_{\bar{x}}} = \dfrac{150 - 153.7}{1.8410} \approx -2.010 \Rightarrow$

$P(\bar{x} > 150) = normalcdf\left(-2.010, 1*10^{99}\right)$

≈ 0.9778

29) a) This problem states that the population, or x, is normally distributed, so we can use area under the normal curve to find the requested probability.

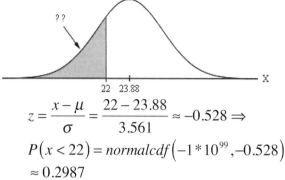

$z = \dfrac{x - \mu}{\sigma} = \dfrac{22 - 23.88}{3.561} \approx -0.528 \Rightarrow$

$P(x < 22) = normalcdf\left(-1*10^{99}, -0.528\right)$

≈ 0.2987

b) Since the population is normal, the possible values of $\bar{x}$ are normal (regardless of the sample size) with $\mu_{\bar{x}} = \mu = 23.88$

and $\sigma_{\bar{x}} \approx \dfrac{3.561}{\sqrt{14}} \approx 0.95172$.

c) This time, we must use $\mu_{\bar{x}}$ and $\sigma_{\bar{x}}$ to calculate the z-scores.

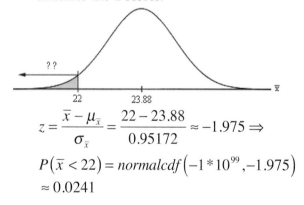

$z = \dfrac{\bar{x} - \mu_{\bar{x}}}{\sigma_{\bar{x}}} = \dfrac{22 - 23.88}{0.95172} \approx -1.975 \Rightarrow$

$P(\bar{x} < 22) = normalcdf\left(-1*10^{99}, -1.975\right)$

≈ 0.0241

31) The problem states that the population is normal with $\mu = 200$ and $\sigma = 10.48$.

a) Questions about a single randomly selected can are questions about the population.

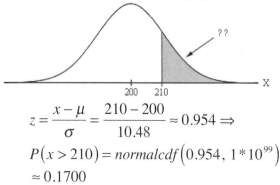

$z = \dfrac{x - \mu}{\sigma} = \dfrac{210 - 200}{10.48} \approx 0.954 \Rightarrow$

$P(x > 210) = normalcdf\left(0.954, 1*10^{99}\right)$

≈ 0.1700

b) Since the population is normal, $\bar{x}$ is normal (regardless of the sample size) with

$$\mu_{\bar{x}} = \mu = 200 \text{ and } \sigma_{\bar{x}} \approx \frac{10.48}{\sqrt{15}} \approx 2.7059$$

c) This time, we must use $\mu_{\bar{x}}$ and $\sigma_{\bar{x}}$ to calculate the z-scores.

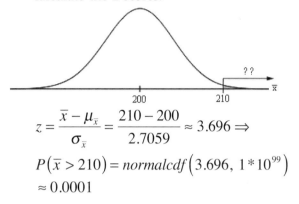

$$z = \frac{\bar{x} - \mu_{\bar{x}}}{\sigma_{\bar{x}}} = \frac{210 - 200}{2.7059} \approx 3.696 \Rightarrow$$

$$P(\bar{x} > 210) = normalcdf(3.696, 1*10^{99})$$

$$\approx 0.0001$$

33) The population has an unknown distribution with $\mu = 2.559$ and $\sigma = 0.3427$.

a) Since n = 45 ≥ 30, $\bar{x}$ is normal with
$$\mu_{\bar{x}} = \mu = 2.559 \text{ and }$$
$$\sigma_{\bar{x}} \approx \frac{0.3427}{\sqrt{45}} \approx 0.051087.$$

b) No assumptions are needed since the sample size is ≥ 30, $\bar{x}$ is normal regardless of the distribution of the population.

c) To say that the sampling error is less than $0.05 means that the value of $\bar{x}$ lies within $0.05 of the true mean of the population. So, we are looking for

$$P(\mu - 0.05 < \bar{x} < \mu + 0.05)$$

$$= P(2.509 < \bar{x} < 2.609).$$

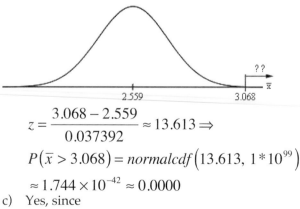

$$z_1 = \frac{2.509 - 2.559}{0.051087} \approx -0.979 \text{ and}$$

$$z_2 = \frac{2.609 - 2.559}{0.051087} \approx 0.979 \Rightarrow$$

$$P(2.509 < \bar{x} < 2.609) =$$

$$normalcdf(-0.979, 0.979) \approx 0.6724$$

d) Increasing n will decrease $\sigma_{\bar{x}}$ which will, in turn, increase the z-scores and thus the probability.

e) We are still trying to find $P(2.509 < \bar{x} < 2.609)$, but the value of $\sigma_{\bar{x}}$ has changed due to the increased sample size. $\sigma_{\bar{x}} \approx \frac{0.3427}{\sqrt{500}} \approx 0.015326$

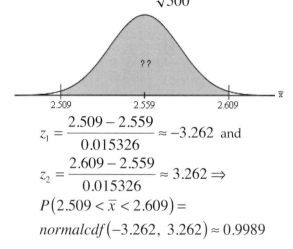

$$z_1 = \frac{2.509 - 2.559}{0.015326} \approx -3.262 \text{ and}$$

$$z_2 = \frac{2.609 - 2.559}{0.015326} \approx 3.262 \Rightarrow$$

$$P(2.509 < \bar{x} < 2.609) =$$

$$normalcdf(-3.262, 3.262) \approx 0.9989$$

35) If $\mu = 2.559$, $\sigma = 0.3427$, and $n = 84$, then $\bar{x}$ is normally distributed (since $n = 84 \geq 30$) with $\mu_{\bar{x}} = \mu = 2.559$ and

$$\sigma_{\bar{x}} \approx \frac{0.3427}{\sqrt{84}} \approx 0.037392.$$

a) $z = \frac{3.068 - 2.559}{0.037392} \approx 13.613 \Rightarrow$ Yes, in fact, it would be very unusual because it would be more than 3 standard deviations away from the mean.

b) We need to find $P(\bar{x} > 3.068)$.

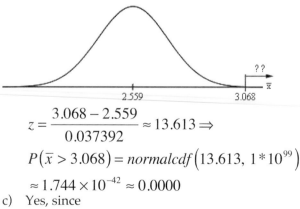

$$z = \frac{3.068 - 2.559}{0.037392} \approx 13.613 \Rightarrow$$

$$P(\bar{x} > 3.068) = normalcdf(13.613, 1*10^{99})$$

$$\approx 1.744 \times 10^{-42} \approx 0.0000$$

c) Yes, since
$$P(\bar{x} \geq 3.068) = 1.744 \times 10^{-42} \approx 0.0000, \text{ it}$$
would be nearly impossible to get such an $\bar{x}$ in California if $\mu = 2.559$ and $\sigma = 0.3427$ in California.

Section 7.4:

37) If $np \geq 5$ and $nq \geq 5$, then $\hat{p}$ will be __normally__ distributed.

39) $n = 200$, $p = 0.784 \Rightarrow q = 0.216$

a) $np = 156.8 \geq 5$ and $nq = 43.2 \geq 5$, so $\hat{p}$ is normally distributed with
$$\mu_{\hat{p}} = p = 0.784$$
and $\sigma_{\hat{p}} = \sqrt{\dfrac{0.784 * 0.216}{200}} \approx 0.029098$.

b) We must remember to use $\mu_{\hat{p}}$ and $\sigma_{\hat{p}}$ when calculating z-scores for $\hat{p}$.

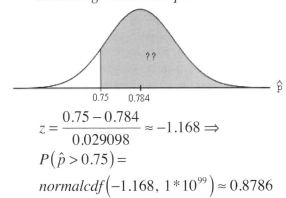

$$z = \frac{0.75 - 0.784}{0.029098} \approx -1.168 \Rightarrow$$
$$P(\hat{p} > 0.75) =$$
$$normalcdf\left(-1.168,\ 1 * 10^{99}\right) \approx 0.8786$$

c) We want to be within 0.05 of the population proportion. This translates to
$$P(0.784 - .05 < \hat{p} < 0.784 + 0.05) =$$
$$P(0.734 < \hat{p} < 0.834).$$

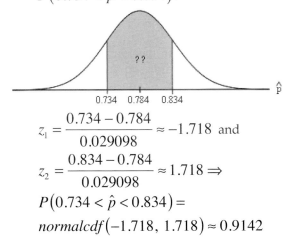

$$z_1 = \frac{0.734 - 0.784}{0.029098} \approx -1.718 \text{ and}$$
$$z_2 = \frac{0.834 - 0.784}{0.029098} \approx 1.718 \Rightarrow$$
$$P(0.734 < \hat{p} < 0.834) =$$
$$normalcdf(-1.718, 1.718) \approx 0.9142$$

41) $n = 600$, $p = 0.37 \Rightarrow q = 0.63$

a) $np = 222 \geq 5$ and $nq = 378 \geq 5$, so the possible values of $\hat{p}$ are normally distributed with $\mu_{\hat{p}} = p = 0.37$
and $\sigma_{\hat{p}} = \sqrt{\dfrac{0.37 * 0.63}{600}} \approx 0.019710$.

b) Examining the graph of $P(\hat{p} < 0.35 \text{ or } \hat{p} > 0.40)$ shown below, we see that the two parts do not overlap. Therefore, we can find each area separately and then add the two values together.

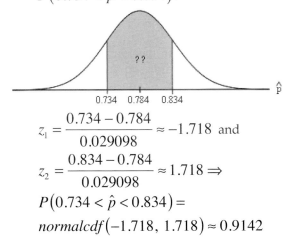

$$z_1 = \frac{0.35 - 0.37}{0.019710} \approx -1.015 \Rightarrow$$
$$P(\hat{p} < 0.35) =$$
$$normalcdf\left(-1 * 10^{99},\ -1.015\right) \approx 0.1551$$
$$z_2 = \frac{0.40 - 0.37}{0.019710} \approx 1.522 \Rightarrow$$
$$P(\hat{p} > 0.40) =$$
$$normalcdf\left(1.522,\ 1 * 10^{99}\right) \approx 0.0640$$

Finally, we get our result by adding these two values together.
$$P(\hat{p} < 0.35 \text{ or } \hat{p} > 0.40) \approx$$
$$0.1551 + 0.0640 = 0.2191$$

Note: We could have also found this by finding the area between 0.35 and 0.40 and subtracting it from 1.

c) For this one, we can use the conditional probability rule. $P(A|B) = \dfrac{P(A \,\&\, B)}{P(B)} \Rightarrow$

$P(\hat{p} < 0.35 | \hat{p} \le 0.40) =$

$\dfrac{P(\hat{p} < 0.35 \,\&\, \hat{p} \le 0.40)}{P(\hat{p} \le 0.40)}$

We can simplify the numerator by noting that & means 'overlap'. Examining the graph below, we see that the overlap is the region to the left of 0.35.

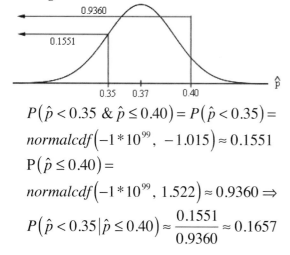

$P(\hat{p} < 0.35 \,\&\, \hat{p} \le 0.40) = P(\hat{p} < 0.35) =$

$normalcdf\left(-1 * 10^{99},\ -1.015\right) \approx 0.1551$

$P(\hat{p} \le 0.40) =$

$normalcdf\left(-1 * 10^{99},\ 1.522\right) \approx 0.9360 \Rightarrow$

$P(\hat{p} < 0.35 | \hat{p} \le 0.40) \approx \dfrac{0.1551}{0.9360} \approx 0.1657$

43) $n = 40$, $p = 0.768 \Rightarrow q = 0.232$

a) $np = 30.72 \ge 5$ and $nq = 9.28 \ge 5$, so the possible values of $\hat{p}$ are normally distributed with $\mu_{\hat{p}} = p = 0.768$ and

$\sigma_{\hat{p}} = \sqrt{\dfrac{0.768 * 0.232}{40}} \approx 0.066741$.

b) $z = \dfrac{0.70 - 0.768}{0.066741} \approx -1.019$. No, 70% is less than 2 standard deviations below the expected proportion, so it would not be considered unusual.

c) In symbols this translates to $P(\hat{p} \le 0.70)$.

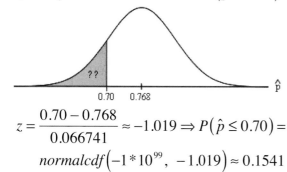

$z = \dfrac{0.70 - 0.768}{0.066741} \approx -1.019 \Rightarrow P(\hat{p} \le 0.70) =$

$normalcdf\left(-1 * 10^{99},\ -1.019\right) \approx 0.1541$

45) $n = 150$, $p = 0.5 \Rightarrow q = 0.5$

a) $np = 75 \ge 5$ and $nq = 75 \ge 5$, so $\hat{p}$ is normally distributed with $\mu_{\hat{p}} = p = 0.5$ and $\sigma_{\hat{p}} = \sqrt{\dfrac{0.5 * 0.5}{150}} \approx 0.040825$.

b) The expected error is anything less than $2\sigma_{\hat{p}} \approx 0.081650$.

c) In symbols, this translates as follows:

$P(0.50 - 0.02 < \hat{p} < 0.50 + 0.02)$

$= P(0.48 < \hat{p} < 0.52)$

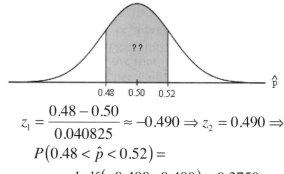

$z_1 = \dfrac{0.48 - 0.50}{0.040825} \approx -0.490 \Rightarrow z_2 = 0.490 \Rightarrow$

$P(0.48 < \hat{p} < 0.52) =$

$normalcdf\left(-0.490,\ 0.490\right) \approx 0.3759$

d) It should increase it, since larger n implies a smaller $\sigma_{\hat{p}}$. This means that more of the area will be in a smaller area surrounding the true value of p.

e) This is the same question as part (c), so we again are trying to find $P(0.48 < \hat{p} < 0.52)$. However, this time we must use $\sigma_{\hat{p}} = \sqrt{\dfrac{0.5 * 0.5}{650}} \approx 0.019612$.

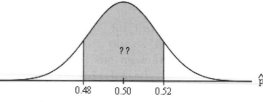

$z_1 = \dfrac{0.48 - 0.50}{0.019612} \approx -1.020 \Rightarrow z_2 = 1.020 \Rightarrow$

$P(0.48 < \hat{p} < 0.52) =$

$normalcdf\left(-1.020,\ 1.020\right) \approx 0.6923$

Chapter Problem:

The problem states that the standard deviation of all such cans is 0.2306 oz. Because this value is for all the cans, it is the population standard deviation, σ. The say the sample size will be 40 cans, so $n = 40$.

a) $\mu_{\bar{x}} = \mu = 12$ and

$$\sigma_{\bar{x}} \approx \frac{\sigma}{\sqrt{n}} = \frac{0.2306}{\sqrt{40}} \approx 0.036461$$

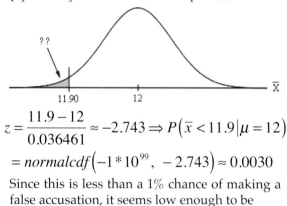

Since we want exactly the left half of the area under the curve, we know the area is 0.5 without using z-scores or normalcdf.

$$P(\bar{x} < 12 | \mu = 12) = 0.5$$

b) No, since n = 40 ≥ 30, we know that $\bar{x}$ will be normally distributed regardless of the distribution of the population.

c) $\mu_{\bar{x}}$ and $\sigma_{\bar{x}}$ are the same as in part (a).

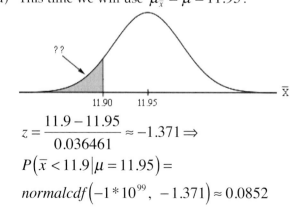

$$z = \frac{11.9 - 12}{0.036461} \approx -2.743 \Rightarrow P(\bar{x} < 11.9 | \mu = 12)$$

$$= normalcdf(-1*10^{99}, -2.743) \approx 0.0030$$

Since this is less than a 1% chance of making a false accusation, it seems low enough to be acceptable.

d) This time we will use $\mu_{\bar{x}} = \mu = 11.95$.

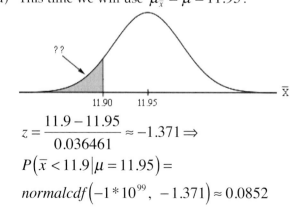

$$z = \frac{11.9 - 11.95}{0.036461} \approx -1.371 \Rightarrow$$

$$P(\bar{x} < 11.9 | \mu = 11.95) =$$

$$normalcdf(-1*10^{99}, -1.371) \approx 0.0852$$

There is only an 8.52% chance that our sample will provide a sample mean low enough for us to make an accusation against the company. So, even though they are cheating us a little bit, they will probably get away with it.

Cumulative Review: Chapters 5 – 7

1) a) $\left\{-0.5841, \frac{7}{2}, 1.604\right\}$ because probabilities must be between 0 and 1 inclusive. $0 \le P(E) \le 1$

   b) This helps us catch errors. If we get an answer that is negative or larger than 1, we need to look for a mistake in our work.

2) a) $\frac{8}{64} = 0.125$

   b) $\frac{3+6+5}{64} = \frac{14}{64} = 0.21875$

   c) $\frac{64-26}{64} = \frac{38}{64} = 0.59375$

   d) $\frac{5}{64} \cdot \frac{7}{63} \approx 0.0087$

   e) Note: Since nor order is specified, we must calculate all possible orders and then add.

   $$\frac{4}{64} \cdot \frac{8}{63} + \frac{8}{64} \cdot \frac{4}{63} \approx 0.0159$$

   f) $\frac{26}{64} \cdot \frac{25}{63} \cdot \frac{24}{62} \cdot \frac{23}{61} \approx 0.0235$

   g) Note: It doesn't say which artist, so we must calculate this for all possible artists and then add the results.

   $$\frac{5}{64} \cdot \frac{4}{63} + \frac{8}{64} \cdot \frac{7}{63} + \ldots + \frac{4}{64} \cdot \frac{3}{63} \approx 0.2073$$

3) a) We should make a chart to show all the possible sums. However, since the coins are chosen without replacement, the same exact coin can't be chosen twice. This is way the diagonal is shaded out.

	0.01	0.01	0.05	0.10	0.25	0.25
0.01		0.02	0.06	0.11	0.26	0.26
0.01	0.02		0.06	0.11	0.26	0.26
0.05	0.06	0.06		0.15	0.30	0.30
0.10	0.11	0.11	0.15		0.35	0.35
0.25	0.26	0.26	0.30	0.35		0.50
0.25	0.26	0.26	0.30	0.35	0.50	

Filling in the chart below is just a matter of counting the possible ways a sum can occur. For example,

$$P(X = 0.35) = \frac{4}{30} \approx 0.1333.$$

x	0.02	0.06	0.11	0.15	0.26	0.30	0.35	0.50
P(x)	.0667	.1333	.1333	.0667	.2667	.1333	.1333	.0667

b) $\dfrac{20}{30} \approx 0.6667$

c) Recall: '&' means overlap, so

$P(X > 0.25 \ \& \ X < 0.50)$ becomes

$P(0.25 < X < 0.50)$. $\dfrac{16}{30} \approx 0.5333$

d) To computer an 'OR' we should count everything from the first event and then anything new from the second one. So we get $\dfrac{18+6}{30} = 0.8$.

e) For a conditional probability, we want to make the given the new sample space. There are 18 possibilities where at least 1 penny is chosen and 8 of those are at least 0.15. So, we get $\dfrac{8}{18} \approx 0.4444$.

f) This time the new sample space is the 18 possibilities that contain at least one quarter. Of course, all 18 of those are at least 0.15, so we get $\dfrac{18}{18} = 1$.

g) We need to make a table to get the needed sums.

x	$P(x)$	$xP(x)$	$(x - \mu_x)^2 P(x)$
0.02	0.0667	0.001334	0.002758
0.06	0.1333	0.007998	0.003556
0.11	0.1333	0.014663	0.001712
0.15	0.0667	0.010005	0.000359
0.26	0.2667	0.069342	0.000358
0.30	0.1333	0.039990	0.000783
0.35	0.1333	0.046655	0.002139
0.50	0.0667	0.033350	0.005105
		0.223337	0.016770

$\mu_x = \sum xP(x) = 0.223337$ and

$\sigma_x = \sqrt{\sum (x - \mu_x)^2 P(x)} = \sqrt{0.01677}$
≈ 0.12950

h) $z = \dfrac{0.50 - 0.223337}{0.12950} \approx 2.136 \Rightarrow$ Yes, because \$0.50 is more than 2 standard deviations away from the mean.

i) $\mu_x - 2\sigma_x \approx -0.035$ and $\mu_x + 2\sigma_x \approx 0.48$. Therefore, anywhere from 0.02 to 0.35 would be in the expected range.

4) a)

	B1	B2	B3	Total
A1	86	215	184	485
A2	99	152	149	400
A3	216	190	207	613
A4	151	203	148	502
Total	552	760	688	2000

b) $P(A1) = \dfrac{485}{2000} = 0.2425$

c) We just count the overlap of the two requested events.

$$P(A3 \ \& \ B1) = \frac{216}{2000} = 0.1080$$

d) For this 'OR' question, I will count all of B2 and then add anything new from A4.

$$P(A4 \text{ or } B2) = \frac{760 + 151 + 148}{2000} = 0.5295$$

e) 'not B1' means that it must be B2 or B3. So I just count the overlap of A4 with (B2 or B3).

$$P(A4 \text{ & not } B1) = \frac{203 + 148}{2000} = 0.1755$$

f) For this one, the 400 items in the given A2 become our new sample space. Of those 400, 152 of them are B2. So we get $\frac{152}{400} = 0.38$.

g) $P(B2) = \frac{760}{2000} = 0.38 = P(B2|A2) \Rightarrow Yes,$

they are independent events.

h) We need to find the probabilities with a given and without a given to compare and decide. $P(A4|B3) = \frac{148}{688} \approx 0.2151$ and

$P(A4) = \frac{502}{2000} = 0.251$. Since

$P(A4|B3) \neq P(A4)$, then NO, they are not independent.

5) a) $P(C \text{ or } D) = P(C) + P(D) - P(C \text{ & } D)$
$= 0.4128 + 0.7355 - 0.3389 = 0.8094$

b) $P(\text{not } D) = 1 - P(D) = 1 - 0.7355 = 0.2645$

c) $P(C|D) = \frac{P(C \text{ & } D)}{P(D)} = \frac{0.3389}{0.7355} \approx 0.4608$

d) $P(D|C) = \frac{P(C \text{ & } D)}{P(C)} = \frac{0.3389}{0.4128} \approx 0.8210$

6) a) Because the problem states that E and F are independent. We can use the special multiplication rule.

$$P(E \text{ & } F) = P(E) \cdot P(F) = \frac{3}{4} \cdot \frac{5}{8} = 0.46875$$

b) $P(E \text{ or } F) = P(E) + P(F) - P(E \text{ & } F)$

$= \frac{3}{4} + \frac{5}{8} - \frac{15}{32} = 0.90625$

7) a) Two events, A and B, are mutually exclusive iff $P(A \text{ & } B) = 0$.

$$P(A \text{ or } B) = P(A) + P(B) - P(A \text{ & } B) \Rightarrow$$

$$\frac{3}{4} = \frac{1}{4} + \frac{1}{2} - P(A \text{ & } B) \Rightarrow$$

$$P(A \text{ & } B) = \frac{1}{4} + \frac{1}{2} - \frac{3}{4} = 0$$

Yes, A and B are mutually exclusive because $P(A \text{ & } B) = 0$.

b) A and B are independent iff $P(A|B) = P(A)$.

$$P(A|B) = \frac{P(A \text{ & } B)}{P(B)} = \frac{0}{P(B)} = 0 \Rightarrow$$

No, A and B are not independent because $P(A|B) \neq P(A)$.

8) a) Coin flips and dice rolls are all independent events, so we can use the special multiplication rule.

$$P(HH444) = \frac{1}{2} \cdot \frac{1}{2} \cdot \frac{1}{6} \cdot \frac{1}{6} \cdot \frac{1}{6} \approx 0.0011574$$

b) This time, the question does not specify which side of the coins comes up or what number is on the die. When the problem does not specify such things, we must add the probabilities for all the possibilities.

$$P(HH111) + P(HH222) + \ldots + P(TT666)$$

$$= 12 \cdot \frac{1}{2} \cdot \frac{1}{2} \cdot \frac{1}{6} \cdot \frac{1}{6} \cdot \frac{1}{6} \approx 0.0139$$

9) We are counting the number of successes in 5 tries, so this is a binomial distribution.

a) $n = 5$ and $p = 0.849 \Rightarrow q = 0.151$

b) $P(X = 3) = \binom{5}{3}(0.849)^3 (0.151)^2 \approx$

0.1395

c) We need the probabilities for all the different values of X. So, we repeat the use of the binomial formula.
Calculator Tip: Enter the work from part (b) all in one line on your calculator, then press 2ND and ENTER to allow you to edit your previous entry.

$$P(0) = \binom{5}{0}(0.849)^0 (0.151)^5 \approx 0.0001$$

$$P(1) = \binom{5}{1}(0.849)^1 (0.151)^4 \approx 0.0022$$

$$P(2) = \binom{5}{2}(0.849)^2 (0.151)^5 \approx 0.0248$$

$$P(4) = \binom{5}{4}(0.849)^4 (0.151)^1 \approx 0.3923$$

$$P(5) = \binom{5}{5}(0.849)^5 (0.151)^0 \approx 0.4411$$

x	0	1	2	3	4	5
$P(x)$	.0001	.0022	.0248	.1395	.3923	.4411

d) Because this is a binomial distribution, we can use the shortcut formulas.
$\mu_x = np = 5 * 0.849 = 4.245$;
$\sigma_x = \sqrt{npq} = \sqrt{5 * 0.849 * 0.151} \approx 0.80062$

10) We are counting the number of successes in 15 households, so this is a binomial distribution with $n = 15$, $p = 0.329$, and $q = 0.671$.

a) $P(6) = \binom{15}{6}(0.329)^6 (0.671)^9 \approx 0.1750$

b) $P(4 \le X < 8) = P(4) + P(5) + P(6) + P(7)$
$= 0.1985 + 0.2142 + 0.1750 + 0.1103 = 0.6980$

c) $P(X \ge 2) = 1 - P(0) - P(1) \approx$
$1 - 0.0025 - 0.0185 = 0.9790$

d) $\mu_x = np = 15 * 0.329 = 4.935$;
$\sigma_x = \sqrt{npq} = \sqrt{15 * 0.329 * 0.671} \approx 1.8197$

e) $\mu_x - 2\sigma_x \approx 1.29$ and $\mu_x + 2\sigma_x \approx 8.57 \Rightarrow$ Anywhere from 2 to 8 households.

11) a) This one is NOT a binomial r.v. because it is the weight of a single apple, not the number of successes out of many.

b) This one is binomial because it counts the number of successes (defectives) out of many sampled bulbs.

c) This one is binomial because it counts the number of successes (sums larger than 9) out of 80 rolls.

d) The one is NOT a binomial r.v. because it is the sum of the dice after one roll, not the number of successes after many rolls.

e) It is important to recognize a binomial r.v., because these are the n, p, q problems where we must use the "n choose x" formula to calculate probabilities and can use the shortcut formulas for finding the mean and standard deviation.

12) a) The sketch indicates a small area should be expected.

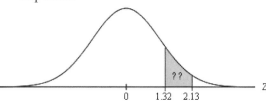

$Area = normalcdf(1.32, 2.13) \approx 0.0768$

b) The sketch indicates an area close to 1.

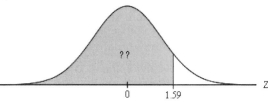

$Area = normalcdf(-1 * 10^{99}, 1.59) \approx 0.9441$

c) We want any part of the curve that is covered by at least 1 of the two arrows shown on the sketch below.

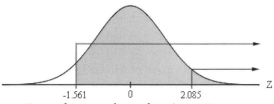

Everything to the right of −1.561 is covered by at least one of the arrows.
$P(z > -1.561 \text{ or } z \ge 2.085) =$
$normalcdf(-1.561, 1 * 10^{99}) \approx 0.9407$

d) This time we want the overlapping part of the two arrows on the sketch below.

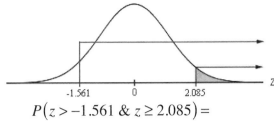

$$P(z > -1.561 \ \& \ z \geq 2.085) =$$

$$normalcdf(2.085, \ 1 * 10^{99}) \approx 0.0185$$

e) If the area in the middle is 0.84, then that leaves $1 - 0.84 = 0.16$ to split between the two sides. So each side gets 0.08. See the sketch below.

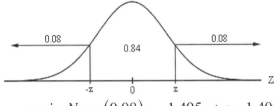

$$-z = invNorm(0.08) \approx -1.405 \Rightarrow z \approx 1.405$$

f) The area to the right is 0.17, so the area to the left is 0.83. See sketch below.

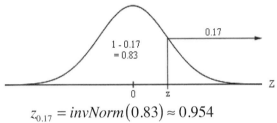

$$z_{0.17} = invNorm(0.83) \approx 0.954$$

g) The area to the right is 0.71, so the area to the left is 0.29. See sketch below.

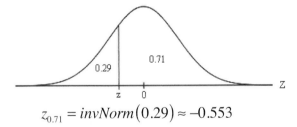

$$z_{0.71} = invNorm(0.29) \approx -0.553$$

13) The population is normal with $\mu = 24.3$ and $\sigma = 5.581$.

a) We want the area to the right of 30.

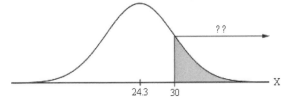

$$z = \frac{30 - 24.3}{5.581} \approx 1.021 \Rightarrow$$

$$Area = normalcdf(1.021, \ 1 * 10^{99}) \approx 0.1536$$

So, we can say that 15.36% of rainbow trout are longer than 30 inches.

b) The percentile number gives us the area to the left of the X value we are looking for. So the area to the left is 0.98. See sketch.

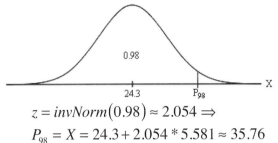

$$z = invNorm(0.98) \approx 2.054 \Rightarrow$$

$$P_{98} = X = 24.3 + 2.054 * 5.581 \approx 35.76$$

c) 98% of mature rainbow trout have lengths less than 35.76 inches.

14) a) For a normally distributed random variable, we simply use the corresponding area under the normal curve for probability.

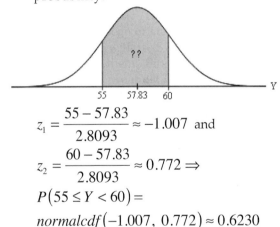

$$z_1 = \frac{55 - 57.83}{2.8093} \approx -1.007 \text{ and}$$

$$z_2 = \frac{60 - 57.83}{2.8093} \approx 0.772 \Rightarrow$$

$$P(55 \leq Y < 60) =$$

$$normalcdf(-1.007, \ 0.772) \approx 0.6230$$

Note: Since Y is a continuous variable, it doesn't matter whether or not the endpoints are included.

b) For an 'OR' question, we want to take all the area from one part and add any new area from the other. Since these two areas are mutually exclusive, we just find the areas and add them together.

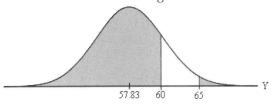

$$z_1 = \frac{60 - 57.83}{2.8093} \approx 0.772 \text{ and}$$

$$z_2 = \frac{65 - 57.83}{2.8093} \approx 2.552 \Rightarrow$$

$normalcdf\left(-1 * 10^{99}, \; 0.772\right) \approx 0.7799$

$normalcdf\left(2.552, \; 1 * 10^{99}\right) \approx 0.0054$

$P\left(Y < 60 \text{ or } Y \geq 65\right) \approx$

$0.7799 + 0.0054 = 0.7853$

c) For this one, we will use the conditional probability rule. So we get:

$$P\left(Y \geq 55 \middle| Y \leq 60\right) = \frac{P\left(Y \geq 55 \;\&\; Y \leq 60\right)}{P\left(Y \leq 60\right)}$$

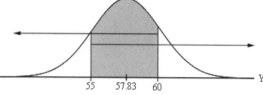

For the '&', we use the overlap from the graph above. So, we want to find

$P\left(55 \leq Y \leq 60\right)$

$= normalcdf\left(-1.007, \; 0.772\right) \approx 0.6230$.

Also, $P\left(Y \leq 60\right) =$

$normalcdf\left(-1 * 10^{99}, \; 0.772\right) \approx 0.7799$.

So, putting it all together, we get:

$$P\left(Y \geq 55 \middle| Y \leq 60\right) = \frac{P\left(55 \leq Y \leq 60\right)}{P\left(Y \leq 60\right)} \approx$$

$$\frac{0.6230}{0.7799} \approx 0.7988$$

d) This is a working backwards question because we are told that the area to the right of k is 0.05. See sketch below.

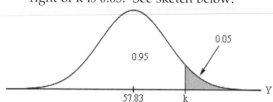

$z = invNorm\left(0.95\right) \approx 1.645 \Rightarrow$

$k = 57.83 + 1.645 * 2.8093 \approx 62.45$

15) We are counting the number of successes in 480 trials, so this is a binomial distribution with $n = 480$, $p = 0.391$, and $q = 0.609$. Since we will be using the normal approximation, we must know the mean and standard deviation.

$\mu_X = np = 187.68$ and $\sigma_X = \sqrt{npq} \approx 10.691$.

a) We want to approximate this probability by approximating the area of the histogram bar for 200. See sketch below.

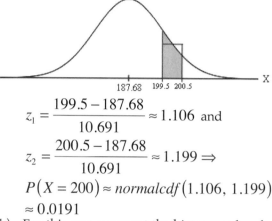

$$z_1 = \frac{199.5 - 187.68}{10.691} \approx 1.106 \text{ and}$$

$$z_2 = \frac{200.5 - 187.68}{10.691} \approx 1.199 \Rightarrow$$

$P\left(X = 200\right) \approx normalcdf\left(1.106, \; 1.199\right)$

≈ 0.0191

b) For this one, we want the histogram bar for 200 and all the bars to the right.

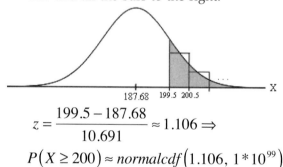

$$z = \frac{199.5 - 187.68}{10.691} \approx 1.106 \Rightarrow$$

$P\left(X \geq 200\right) \approx normalcdf\left(1.106, \; 1 * 10^{99}\right)$

≈ 0.1344

c) $np = 187.68 \geq 5$ and $nq = 292.32 \geq 5$, so the requirements have been met.

16) a) Entering the data values in L1 and choosing STAT > CALC > 1-Var Stats L1, we obtain $\mu = 47$ and $\sigma \approx 8.3367$.

b) {47,37,44},{47,37,60},{47,44,60},{37,44,60}

c) Each sample mean is found by adding the three values and dividing by 3. For example, the first one is given by

$$\bar{x} = \frac{\sum x}{n} = \frac{47 + 37 + 44}{3} \approx 42.67$$

Since there are four samples possible, each sample and sample mean has a $1/4 = 0.25$ chance of occurring.

$\bar{x}$	42.67	48	50.33	47
P($\bar{x}$)	.25	.25	.25	.25

d) $P(\mu - 4 < \bar{x} < \mu + 4) = P(43 < \bar{x} < 51) =$

$$\frac{3}{4} = 0.75$$

Note: Since there are only 4 samples possible, we simply count how many of them have values of $\bar{x}$ in the desired range.

17) a) $\bar{x}$ is normally distributed with
$$\mu_{\bar{x}} = \mu = 41.93 \ \&$$
$$\sigma_{\bar{x}} = \frac{8.2771}{\sqrt{47}} \approx 1.2073.$$

b) Remember: Since this is a probability question about $\bar{x}$, we must use $\mu_{\bar{x}}$ and $\sigma_{\bar{x}}$ when calculating the z-scores.

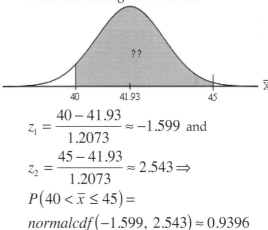

$$z_1 = \frac{40 - 41.93}{1.2073} \approx -1.599 \text{ and}$$

$$z_2 = \frac{45 - 41.93}{1.2073} \approx 2.543 \Rightarrow$$

$$P(40 < \bar{x} \le 45) =$$

$$normalcdf(-1.599, 2.543) \approx 0.9396$$

c) This means we want $\bar{x}$ to be within 3 units of the true mean, 41.93. So we need:

$$P(\mu - 3 < \bar{x} < \mu + 3) = P(38.93 < \bar{x} < 44.93)$$

$$z_1 = \frac{38.93 - 41.93}{1.2073} \approx -2.485 \text{ and}$$

$$z_2 = \frac{44.93 - 41.93}{1.2073} \approx 2.485 \Rightarrow$$

$$P(38.93 < \bar{x} < 44.93) =$$

$$normalcdf(-2.485, 2.485) \approx 0.9870$$

d) No. Since $n = 47 \ge 30$, $\bar{x}$ will be normally distributed regardless of the distribution of the population.

18) This is a success/failure problem with
$$n = 175, \ p = \frac{18}{38}, \text{ and } q = \frac{20}{38}.$$

a) $np = 175 \cdot \dfrac{18}{38} \approx 82.89 \geq 5$ and

$nq = 175 \cdot \dfrac{20}{38} \approx 92.11 \geq 5 \Rightarrow \hat{p}$ is

normally distributed with
$\mu_{\hat{p}} = p \approx 0.473684$

and $\sigma_{\hat{p}} = \sqrt{\dfrac{pq}{n}} \approx 0.037744$.

b) This translates to $P(\hat{p} > 0.50)$. Since $\hat{p}$ is normally distributed, we can answer this using area under a normal curve.

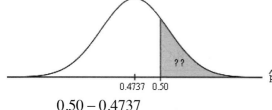

$z = \dfrac{0.50 - 0.4737}{0.037744} \approx 0.697 \Rightarrow$

$P(\hat{p} > 0.50) =$

$normalcdf(0.697, \ 1 * 10^{99}) \approx 0.2429$

c) Translation:
$P(p - 0.02 < \hat{p} < p + 0.02) =$
$P(0.4537 < \hat{p} < 0.4937)$

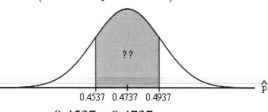

$z_1 = \dfrac{0.4537 - 0.4737}{0.037744} = -0.530$ and

$z_2 = \dfrac{0.4937 - 0.4737}{0.037744} = 0.530 \Rightarrow$

$P(0.4537 < \hat{p} < 0.4937) =$

$normalcdf(-0.530, \ 0.530) \approx 0.4039$

d) $\mu_{\hat{p}} - 2\sigma_{\hat{p}} = 0.473684 - 2 * 0.037744$
$= 0.398196$ and $\mu_{\hat{p}} + 2\sigma_{\hat{p}} =$
$0.473684 + 2 * 0.037744 = 0.549172$.
Therefore, the expected range for the winning percentage is anywhere between 39.8196% and 54.9172%

e) They must try to get the gambler to play more than 175 times. That is, they would want to increase the sample size.

f) $n = 751 \Rightarrow \sigma_{\hat{p}} = \sqrt{\dfrac{pq}{n}} \approx 0.018220$

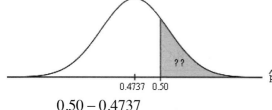

$z = \dfrac{0.50 - 0.4737}{0.018220} \approx 1.443 \Rightarrow$

$P(\hat{p} > 0.50) =$

$normalcdf(1.443, \ 1 * 10^{99}) \approx 0.0745$

Section 8.1:

1) When estimating a population mean, our point estimate will be the <u>sample mean</u>.

2) Because we do not expect our point estimate to be correct, we add and subtract an amount from it to form a confidence interval. The amount added and subtracted is referred to as the <u>margin</u> of <u>error</u>.

3) When we expand our estimate to a confidence interval, the percentage stated is known as the confidence <u>level</u>.

4) When we say we are 95% (or some other %) confident that our interval contains the population mean, this means that in the <u>long run</u>, 95% of such intervals will contain their population mean.

5) The requirement for finding a confidence interval for a mean is that we must have a large <u>sample</u> ($n \geq 30$) OR a normal <u>population</u>.

6) For a fixed sample size, the <u>larger</u> the confidence level, the larger the interval and vice versa.

7) Given information: $n = 42$, $\sigma = 14.05$, $\bar{x} = 81.4$
   a) Since $n = 42 \geq 30$, we know, by the CLT, that $\bar{x}$ will be normally distributed. So, the requirements are satisfied.
   b) 68.27% is the area within 1 standard deviation from the Empirical Rule for normal distributions, so we use the formula
   $$\bar{x} \pm 1 \cdot \frac{\sigma}{\sqrt{n}}$$ to find the boundaries of the confidence interval.
   $$\bar{x} \pm 1 \cdot \frac{\sigma}{\sqrt{n}} = 81.4 \pm 1 \cdot \frac{14.05}{\sqrt{42}} =$$
   $$81.4 \pm 2.2 \Rightarrow \mu \in (79.2, 83.6)$$
   Note: We always match the number of decimal places on the margin of error with the our point estimate, $\bar{x}$.
   c) Because the percentage is now 95.45%, we now want to be within 2 standard deviations of $\bar{x}$.
   $$\bar{x} \pm 2 \cdot \frac{\sigma}{\sqrt{n}} = 81.4 \pm 2 \cdot \frac{14.05}{\sqrt{42}} =$$
   $$81.4 \pm 4.3 \Rightarrow \mu \in (77.1, 85.7)$$

d) Since the percentage is 99.73%, this time we want to be within 3 standard deviations of $\bar{x}$.
   $$\bar{x} \pm 3 \cdot \frac{\sigma}{\sqrt{n}} = 81.4 \pm 3 \cdot \frac{14.05}{\sqrt{42}} =$$
   $$81.4 \pm 6.5 \Rightarrow \mu \in (74.9, 87.9)$$
e) The higher the confidence level, the wider the interval.

9) a) The point estimate for estimating population means is the sample mean. Since they have given us $\sum x^2 = 868,328$ to verify data entry, we should enter the data into L1 on the calculator and then choose STAT > CALC > 1-Var Stats L1. This yields $\bar{x} \approx 212.84$.
   b) No, $P(\bar{x} = \mu) \approx 0$.
   c) Since $15 \leq n = 19 < 30$, we must hope that the population is not severely skewed.
   d) Since we are asked to be 95% confident, we need to find the z-scores that trap an area of 0.95 in the middle with equal outside areas. See the sketch below.

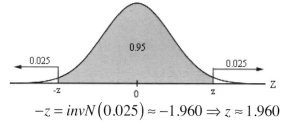

   $$-z = invN(0.025) \approx -1.960 \Rightarrow z \approx 1.960$$
   This is the z-score that we will use in the formula to find our confidence interval boundaries.
   $$\bar{x} \pm 1.96 \cdot \frac{\sigma}{\sqrt{n}} = 212.84 \pm 1.96 \cdot \frac{26}{\sqrt{19}} =$$
   $$212.84 \pm 11.69 \Rightarrow \mu \in (201.15, 224.53)$$
   e) The margin of error is the part we add and subtract from the point estimate. So, the margin of error is 11.69 ft.
   f) I am 95% confident that the mean height of all mature giant sequoias in the grove is somewhere between 201.15 ft and 224.53 ft.
   g) Probably, I am 95% sure that it does. 95% of the time we compute such intervals we capture the true mean, the other 5% to the time we get unlucky and miss.
   h) I would expect about 95% of them to contain the true mean. $0.95 * 200 = 190 \Rightarrow$ About 190 of them should contain the true population mean.

11) Given information: $n = 53$, $\bar{x} = 25.7$, and since the standard deviation is for ALL the students at the school, $\sigma = 11.83$.

a) Since n = 53 ≥ 30, the CLT tells us that $\bar{x}$ will be normally distributed. Thus the requirements have been met.

b) We want an area of 0.99 in the middle with equal outside areas. See the sketch below.

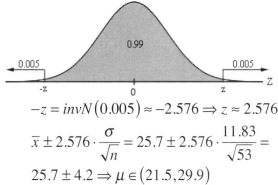

$$-z = invN(0.005) \approx -2.576 \Rightarrow z \approx 2.576$$

$$\bar{x} \pm 2.576 \cdot \frac{\sigma}{\sqrt{n}} = 25.7 \pm 2.576 \cdot \frac{11.83}{\sqrt{53}} =$$

$$25.7 \pm 4.2 \Rightarrow \mu \in (21.5, 29.9)$$

c) I am 99% confident that the mean age of all Chabot students is somewhere between 21.5 and 29.9 years old.

d) The margin of error is 4.2 years. So, I am 99% confident that the population mean is within 4.2 years of my point estimate of 25.7 years old.

13) a) Since n = 34 ≥ 30, the CLT tells us that $\bar{x}$ will be normally distributed. Thus the requirements have been met.

b) We need to calculate the sample mean ourselves, since it was not given. Using the calculator we find $\bar{x} = 17.075$. They state the standard deviation for ALL , so we have $\sigma = 0.703$. For 90% confidence, we need an area of 0.90 in the middle and 0.05 on each side. See sketch below.

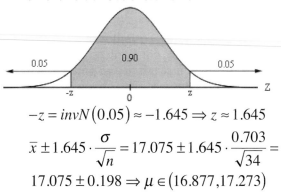

$$-z = invN(0.05) \approx -1.645 \Rightarrow z \approx 1.645$$

$$\bar{x} \pm 1.645 \cdot \frac{\sigma}{\sqrt{n}} = 17.075 \pm 1.645 \cdot \frac{0.703}{\sqrt{34}} =$$

$$17.075 \pm 0.198 \Rightarrow \mu \in (16.877, 17.273)$$

c) I am 90% confident that the mean height of all adult male giraffes is somewhere between 16.877 ft and 17.273 ft.

d) The margin of error is 0.198 ft. So, I am 90% confident that the population mean is within 0.198 ft of my point estimate of 17.075 ft tall.

e) We could decrease our confidence level or we could increase our sample size.

Section 8.2:

15) When we increase our sample size, it decreases the margin of error.

16) When calculating sample size requirements, we always round n up to the next whole number.

17) In cases where σ is unknown, we can replace it by s if we have taken a sample or by the range divided by 4 if we have to guess at it.

18) If we are given a confidence interval, we can obtain the margin of error by dividing the length of the interval by 2 .

19) The point estimate, $\bar{x}$, is the midpoint of the interval and the margin of error is half of the length of the interval. Therefore,

$$\bar{x} = \frac{3.56 + 4.72}{2} = 4.14 \text{ and}$$

$$E = \frac{4.72 - 3.56}{2} = 0.58 .$$

20) We obtain confidence intervals by adding and subtracting the margin of error from the point estimate. $16.09 \pm 0.23 \Rightarrow \mu \in (15.86, 16.32)$

21) We know the population standard deviation is $\sigma = 18.952$ and for 95% confidence, the z-score is found as shown below.

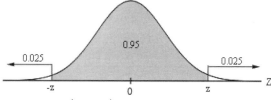

$-z = invN(0.025) \approx -1.960 \Rightarrow z \approx 1.960$

a) The requested margin of error is 2.5, so we know that $E = 2.5$.

$$n = \left(\frac{z\sigma}{E}\right)^2 = \left(\frac{1.96 * 18.952}{2.5}\right)^2 \approx 220.77$$

$\Rightarrow n = 221$ (Always round up.)

b) We will need an even bigger sample.

c) $n = \left(\frac{z\sigma}{E}\right)^2 = \left(\frac{1.96 * 18.952}{1.25}\right)^2 \approx 883.08$

$\Rightarrow n = 884$ (Always round n up.)

23) a) We use the 95% to find the z-score.

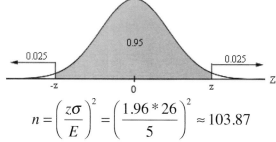

$$n = \left(\frac{z\sigma}{E}\right)^2 = \left(\frac{1.96 * 26}{5}\right)^2 \approx 103.87$$

$\Rightarrow n = 104$ trees need to be sampled.

b) The point estimate is $\bar{x} = 218.9$. This sample size from part (a) will yield $E = 5.0$. We simply add and subtract this from the point estimate to get our interval.

$218.9 \pm 5.0 \Rightarrow \mu \in (213.9, 223.9)$

25) If the population standard deviation, σ, is not given, then the best replacement is the sample standard deviation, s, if it is available. We can use the given sample and the graphing calculator to find the value of s. $s \approx 3.6051$ We use the 90% confidence to find the z-score. **Note**: z-scores (rather than t-scores) are always used when computing sample size.

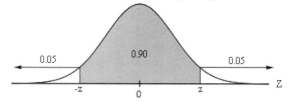

$-z = invN(0.05) \approx -1.645 \Rightarrow z \approx 1.645$

$$n = \left(\frac{z\sigma}{E}\right)^2 \approx \left(\frac{z \cdot s}{E}\right)^2 = \left(\frac{1.645 * 3.6051}{0.5}\right)^2$$

$\approx 140.68 \Rightarrow n = 141$

27) When both the values of σ and s are unavailable, we can estimate σ by using

$$\sigma \approx \frac{max - min}{4} = \frac{3.75 - 3.18}{4} = 0.1425 \,.$$

For 99% confidence the z-scores are:

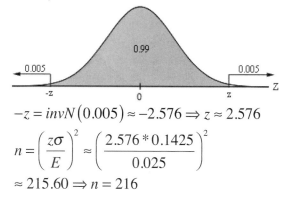

$-z = invN(0.005) \approx -2.576 \Rightarrow z \approx 2.576$

$$n = \left(\frac{z\sigma}{E}\right)^2 \approx \left(\frac{2.576 * 0.1425}{0.025}\right)^2$$

$\approx 215.60 \Rightarrow n = 216$

Section 8.3:

29) t-curves are similar in shape to the z-curve except that they tend to be <u>shorter</u> and <u>wider</u>.

30) As the df increases, t-curves look more and more like the <u>standard</u> <u>normal</u> curve.

31) We must use a t-curve when σ is <u>unknown</u> and we replace it with <u>s</u>.

32) If the df you need is not on the t-table, then you should always round <u>down</u>. This keeps us from <u>over</u> stating our confidence level.

33) a) 1.729   c) 2.650
    b) 1.699   d) 2.576

35) Given information: $n = 76$, $\bar{x} = 18.93$, and $s = 4.078$. This standard deviation came from the sample. That is why it is labeled as s rather than σ.

a) Since n = 76 ≥ 30, the CLT tells us that $\bar{x}$ will be normally distributed. Thus the requirements have been met.

b) Because we do not know the value of σ, we must use t-scores for this problem. We need the two t-scores that trap an area of 0.95 in the middle with equal outside areas.

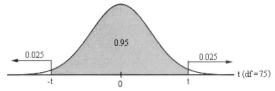

Using the t-table with $df = n - 1 = 75$, we find $t_{0.025} = 1.992$.

$$\bar{x} \pm t \cdot \frac{s}{\sqrt{n}} = 18.93 \pm 1.992 \cdot \frac{4.078}{\sqrt{76}} \approx$$

$$18.93 \pm 0.93 \Rightarrow \mu \in (18.00, 19.86)$$

c) The margin of error is the part we added and subtracted to get the boundaries, therefore, E = 0.93.

37) Given information: $n = 36$, $\bar{x} = 5.62$, and $s = 1.0639$. The standard deviation was obtained from the sample.

a) Since n = 36 ≥ 30, the CLT tells us that $\bar{x}$ will be normally distributed. Thus the requirements have been met.

b) Because we do not know the value of σ, we must use t-scores for this problem.

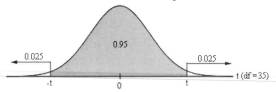

Using the t-table with $df = n - 1 = 35$, we find $t_{0.025} = 2.030$.

$$\bar{x} \pm t \cdot \frac{s}{\sqrt{n}} = 5.62 \pm 2.030 \cdot \frac{1.0639}{\sqrt{36}} \approx$$

$$5.62 \pm 0.36 \Rightarrow \mu \in (5.26, 5.98)$$

c) Yes, $\mu \in (5.26, 5.98) \Rightarrow \mu > 5$.

39) a) Since n = 12 < 15, we must hope that the mileages for all such SUVs is a normally distributed population.

b) We are not given values for the mean or standard deviation, so we will need to compute them from the sample data. Enter the 12 values into L1 and then choose STAT > CALC > 1-Var Stats L1. This yields $\bar{x} \approx 34.573$ and $s \approx 1.6685$.

   Note: The calculator shows values for both σ and s, however, because we entered sample data in, only the value of s is valid and meaningful.

   Because we do not know the value of σ, we must use t-scores for this problem.

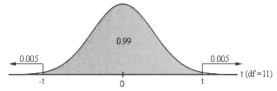

Using the t-table with $df = n - 1 = 11$, we find $t_{0.005} = 3.106$.

$$\bar{x} \pm t \cdot \frac{s}{\sqrt{n}} = 34.573 \pm 3.106 \cdot \frac{1.6685}{\sqrt{12}} \approx$$

$$34.573 \pm 1.496 \Rightarrow \mu \in (33.077, 36.069)$$

c) No, $\mu \in (33.077, 36.069) \Rightarrow \mu$ could be more than 35. For example, it could be 35 mpg.

d) The value of σ is unknown, so we will use s as an approximation for it. A new unknown sample means a new unknown df. Because we can't know what df to use for a t-score, we always use z-scores when computing sample size.

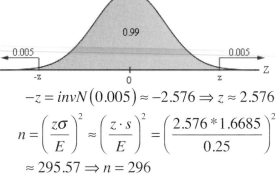

$$-z = invN(0.005) \approx -2.576 \Rightarrow z \approx 2.576$$

$$n = \left(\frac{z\sigma}{E}\right)^2 \approx \left(\frac{z \cdot s}{E}\right)^2 = \left(\frac{2.576 * 1.6685}{0.25}\right)^2$$

$$\approx 295.57 \Rightarrow n = 296$$

e) I don't know. A new sample would produce a new value for $\bar{x}$, and that would completely change the interval. If $\bar{x}$ was less than 34.75, then our interval would show μ was less than 35 mpg.

41) a) Since $n = 48 \geq 30$, $\bar{x}$ will be normal. Thus, the requirements have been met.

b) We must use the sample data to compute the mean and standard deviation. $\bar{x} \approx 28.1$ and $s \approx 10.488$. Because we do not know the value of σ, we must use t-scores for this problem. The actual df is given by $df = n - 1 = 47$, however, this value is not on our table, so we will round down and use $df = 45$.

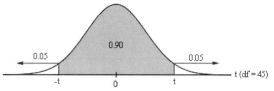

Using the t-table with $df = 45$, we find $t_{0.05} = 1.679$.

$$\bar{x} \pm t \cdot \frac{s}{\sqrt{n}} = 28.1 \pm 1.679 \cdot \frac{10.488}{\sqrt{48}} \approx$$

$$28.1 \pm 2.5 \Rightarrow \mu \in (25.6, \ 30.6)$$

c) Yes, $\mu \in (25.6, \ 30.6) \Rightarrow \mu > 25$

d) We will use s as an approximation for σ. When computing sample size, we always use z-scores.

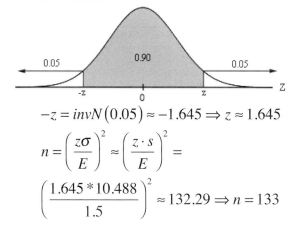

$$-z = invN(0.05) \approx -1.645 \Rightarrow z \approx 1.645$$

$$n = \left(\frac{z\sigma}{E} \right)^2 \approx \left(\frac{z \cdot s}{E} \right)^2 =$$

$$\left(\frac{1.645 * 10.488}{1.5} \right)^2 \approx 132.29 \Rightarrow n = 133$$

Section 8.4:

43) Fill in the blanks: The procedure learned in this section is designed to find confidence intervals for population proportions, but it can also be used to find confidence intervals for <u>percentages</u> and <u>probabilities</u>.

44) Since we do not know the value of p and q, we substitute our best guess for them which would be $\hat{p}$ and $\hat{q}$. So we get the following:

$$np \approx n\hat{p} = n \cdot \frac{x}{n} = x \Rightarrow np \geq 5 \text{ becomes } x \geq 5$$

$$nq \approx n\hat{q} = n \cdot (1 - \hat{p}) = n\left(1 - \frac{x}{n}\right) = n - x \Rightarrow$$

becomes $n - x \geq 5$.

45) Given Info: $n = 318$, $x = 197$

a) The point estimate for a population proportion, p, is the sample proportion, $\hat{p}$.

$$\hat{p} = \frac{197}{318} \approx 0.6195$$

b) $x = 197 \geq 5$ and $n - x = 121 \geq 5$, so the requirements have been met.

c) We always use z-scores for proportion problems. Our confidence level is 95%.

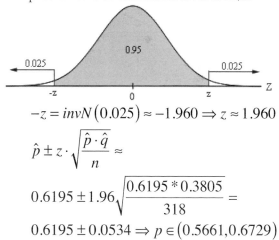

$$-z = invN(0.025) \approx -1.960 \Rightarrow z \approx 1.960$$

$$\hat{p} \pm z \cdot \sqrt{\frac{\hat{p} \cdot \hat{q}}{n}} \approx$$

$$0.6195 \pm 1.96 \sqrt{\frac{0.6195 * 0.3805}{318}} =$$

$$0.6195 \pm 0.0534 \Rightarrow p \in (0.5661, 0.6729)$$

d) The margin of error is the part we add and subtract to get the boundaries. $E = 0.0534$

47) Given Info: $n = 1089$ and $x = 654$

a) The point estimate for a population proportion, p, is the sample proportion, $\hat{p}$.
$$\hat{p} = \frac{654}{1089} \approx 0.6006$$

b) We need the z-scores for 95% confidence.

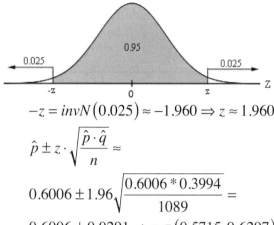

$$-z = invN(0.025) \approx -1.960 \Rightarrow z \approx 1.960$$

$$\hat{p} \pm z \cdot \sqrt{\frac{\hat{p} \cdot \hat{q}}{n}} \approx$$

$$0.6006 \pm 1.96\sqrt{\frac{0.6006 * 0.3994}{1089}} =$$

$$0.6006 \pm 0.0291 \Rightarrow p \in (0.5715, 0.6297)$$

c) Just using the point estimate, we have 0% confidence that we have the true proportion. However, when we add and subtract the margin of error, we become 95% confident that we have captured the true proportion. Therefore, we must be 95% confident that the point estimate is within 0.0291 of the true proportion.

d) We are 95% confident that the true percentage of all registered voters in California who approve of the job the governor is doing is somewhere between 57.15% and 62.97%.

49) Given info: $n = 136$ and $\hat{p} = 0.6250$. Notice: this time, we were given the percentage of successes, $\hat{p}$, rather than the number of successes, x.

a) If we are given $\hat{p}$ rather than x, we can find x by using the formula $x = n\hat{p}$.
$$x = n\hat{p} = 136 * 0.6250 = 85 \geq 5 \text{ and}$$
$n - x = 51 \geq 5$, so the requirements have been met.

b) We need the z-scores for 90% confidence.

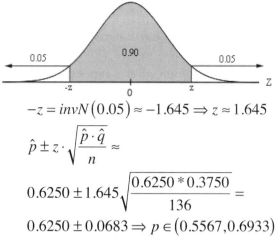

$$-z = invN(0.05) \approx -1.645 \Rightarrow z \approx 1.645$$

$$\hat{p} \pm z \cdot \sqrt{\frac{\hat{p} \cdot \hat{q}}{n}} \approx$$

$$0.6250 \pm 1.645\sqrt{\frac{0.6250 * 0.3750}{136}} =$$

$$0.6250 \pm 0.0683 \Rightarrow p \in (0.5567, 0.6933)$$

c) Yes, $p \in (0.5567, 0.6933) \Rightarrow p > 0.5$

51) Given info: $n = 280$ and $x = 214$

a) $x = 214 \geq 5$ and $n - x = 66 \geq 5$, so the requirements have been met.

b) We need the z-scores for 95% confidence.

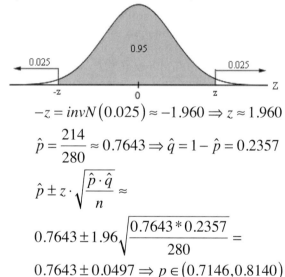

$$-z = invN(0.025) \approx -1.960 \Rightarrow z \approx 1.960$$

$$\hat{p} = \frac{214}{280} \approx 0.7643 \Rightarrow \hat{q} = 1 - \hat{p} = 0.2357$$

$$\hat{p} \pm z \cdot \sqrt{\frac{\hat{p} \cdot \hat{q}}{n}} \approx$$

$$0.7643 \pm 1.96\sqrt{\frac{0.7643 * 0.2357}{280}} =$$

$$0.7643 \pm 0.0497 \Rightarrow p \in (0.7146, 0.8140)$$

Note: We show the zero at the end of 0.8140 because we are supposed to match decimal places with the point estimate.

c) No, $p \in (0.7146, 0.8140) \Rightarrow$ p could be 0.74 which is less than 75%.

53) Given info: $n = 184$ and $\hat{p} = 0.9050$

    a) We need the z-scores for 95% confidence.

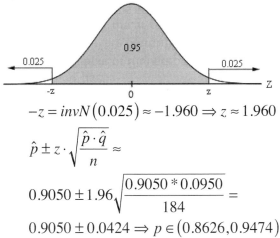

$$-z = invN(0.025) \approx -1.960 \Rightarrow z \approx 1.960$$

$$\hat{p} \pm z \cdot \sqrt{\frac{\hat{p} \cdot \hat{q}}{n}} \approx$$

$$0.9050 \pm 1.96\sqrt{\frac{0.9050 * 0.0950}{184}} =$$

$$0.9050 \pm 0.0424 \Rightarrow p \in (0.8626, 0.9474)$$

    b) We are 95% confident that the proportion of all people classified as allergic to penicillin that can take the drug without an adverse effect is somewhere between 0.8626 and 0.9474.

Section 8.5:

55) When determining the sample size required to obtain a desired margin of error in proportion problems, we must <u>guess</u> at the value of the population proportion.

56) If we have no previous information to help us make a guess at the value of the population proportion, then we should use <u>0.5</u> as our guess.

57) When making a guess at the value of p, we always choose the possibility that is closest to 0.5. This way our sample size is never too small.

    a) $p \in (0.358, 0.444) \Rightarrow p_g = 0.444$

    b) $p \in (0.764, 0.810) \Rightarrow p_g = 0.764$

    c) $p \in (0.457, 0.561) \Rightarrow p_g = 0.5$

Note: On the last one, the interval contained the value of 0.5, so that is the closest value in the interval to 0.5.

59) Given info: We want $E = 0.03$ and for a confidence level of 90%, the z-score are:

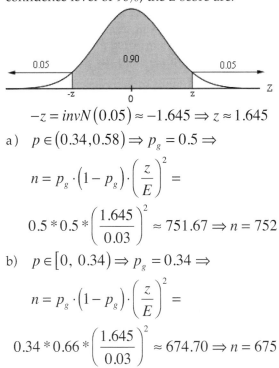

$$-z = invN(0.05) \approx -1.645 \Rightarrow z \approx 1.645$$

    a) $p \in (0.34, 0.58) \Rightarrow p_g = 0.5 \Rightarrow$

$$n = p_g \cdot (1 - p_g) \cdot \left(\frac{z}{E}\right)^2 =$$

$$0.5 * 0.5 * \left(\frac{1.645}{0.03}\right)^2 \approx 751.67 \Rightarrow n = 752$$

    b) $p \in [0, 0.34) \Rightarrow p_g = 0.34 \Rightarrow$

$$n = p_g \cdot (1 - p_g) \cdot \left(\frac{z}{E}\right)^2 =$$

$$0.34 * 0.66 * \left(\frac{1.645}{0.03}\right)^2 \approx 674.70 \Rightarrow n = 675$$

61) Given info: $E = 0.05$ and for a confidence level of 99%, the z-score are:

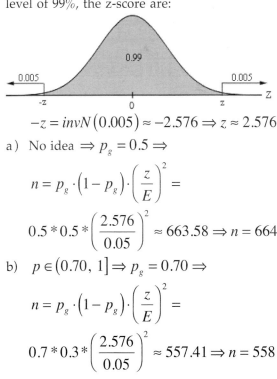

$$-z = invN(0.005) \approx -2.576 \Rightarrow z \approx 2.576$$

    a) No idea $\Rightarrow p_g = 0.5 \Rightarrow$

$$n = p_g \cdot (1 - p_g) \cdot \left(\frac{z}{E}\right)^2 =$$

$$0.5 * 0.5 * \left(\frac{2.576}{0.05}\right)^2 \approx 663.58 \Rightarrow n = 664$$

    b) $p \in (0.70, 1] \Rightarrow p_g = 0.70 \Rightarrow$

$$n = p_g \cdot (1 - p_g) \cdot \left(\frac{z}{E}\right)^2 =$$

$$0.7 * 0.3 * \left(\frac{2.576}{0.05}\right)^2 \approx 557.41 \Rightarrow n = 558$$

63) Let's start by finding the z-scores for 95%
confidence.

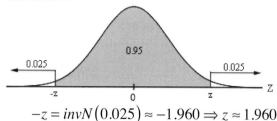

$$-z = invN(0.025) \approx -1.960 \Rightarrow z \approx 1.960$$

a) $p \in (0.5715, 0.6297) \Rightarrow p_g = 0.5715 \Rightarrow$

$$n = p_g \cdot (1 - p_g) \cdot \left(\frac{z}{E}\right)^2 =$$

$$0.5715 * 0.4285 * \left(\frac{1.960}{0.015}\right)^2 \approx 4181.16$$

$$\Rightarrow n = 4182$$

b) No guess at p $\Rightarrow p_g = 0.5 \Rightarrow$

$$n = p_g \cdot (1 - p_g) \cdot \left(\frac{z}{E}\right)^2 =$$

$$0.5 * 0.5 * \left(\frac{1.960}{0.015}\right)^2 \approx 4268.44 \Rightarrow n = 4269$$

Chapter Problem:

a) Given info: $E = 0.1\% = 0.001$.
Probabilities are proportions, so we also
need the z-scores for 99% confidence.

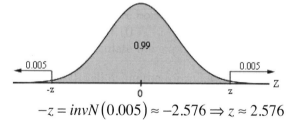

$$-z = invN(0.005) \approx -2.576 \Rightarrow z \approx 2.576$$

The problem states that we are confident
that the true probability is less than 1%.

$$p \in [0, 0.01] \Rightarrow p_g = 0.01 \Rightarrow$$

$$n = p_g \cdot (1 - p_g) \cdot \left(\frac{z}{E}\right)^2 =$$

$$0.01 * 0.99 * \left(\frac{2.576}{0.001}\right)^2 \approx 65,694.18$$

$$\Rightarrow n = 65,695$$

b) $\hat{p} = \frac{x}{n} = \frac{399 + 50 + 56 + 6 + 4}{111637}$

$$\approx 0.00461317$$

c) No, $P(\hat{p} = p) \approx 0$.

Section 9.1

1) H_o must always include the possibility of
equality.

2) The specific value used in H_o is usually an old,
claimed, or comparable value for the mean.

3) A type I error occurs if we reject H_o when it is in
fact a true statement.

4) A type II error occurs if we do not reject H_o
when it is in fact a false statement.

5) a) The claimed or advertised value for the
mean is 22 mpg. They key phrase is that
we wish to show that the mean is actually
"fewer miles per gallon than advertised."
This indicates a less than for H_a.
$H_o : \mu \geq 22$
$H_a : \mu < 22$

b) Since H_a contains a less than, this is a
left-tailed test.

7) a) The claimed value for the mean is 3 grams
of fat per serving. The key phrase is that
he wants to see if the mean is "more grams
. . . than claimed." This indicates a greater
than for H_a.
$H_o : \mu \leq 3$
$H_a : \mu > 3$

b) Since H_a contains a greater than, this is a
right-tailed test.

9) a) The old value for the mean is $6429 per
day. The key phrase is that she want to
determine if the mean has "changed" since
the ads were released. This word does not
indicate a specific direction, so we use does
not equal in H_a.
$H_o : \mu = 6429$
$H_a : \mu \neq 6429$

b) Since H_a contains a does not equal symbol,
this is a two-tailed test.

11) a) The claimed value on the bags is 5 pounds per bag. The key phrase is that we want to detect if the actual mean is "incorrect." This word does not indicate a direction, so we will use a does not equal in H_a.

$H_o : \mu = 5$

$H_a : \mu \neq 5$

b) Since H_a contains a does not equal symbol, this is a two-tailed test.

13) a) The old value for the mean is 65.5 days. The researcher wants to know if the mean is now "different." This word does not indicate a direction, so we will use a does not equal symbol in H_a.

$H_o : \mu = 65.5$

$H_a : \mu \neq 65.5$

b) Since H_a contains the does not equal symbol, this is a two-tailed test.

15) a) To show the mean is higher than 25 points, we start out by using 25 points as a default comparable value for the mean. Since the caller wants to show the mean is "higher" than 25 points, we will use a greater than symbol in H_a.

$H_o : \mu \leq 25$

$H_a : \mu > 25$

b) Since H_a contains a greater than symbol, this is a right-tailed test.

17) Given: $\mu = 22 \Rightarrow H_0 : \mu \geq 22$ is true.

a) Since the research provides insufficient evidence, we will not reject H_0. Putting this decision together with the given, we must have made a Correct Decision.

b) Since the research provides enough evidence, we would reject H_0. Putting this together with the given, we must have made a Type I error.

19) a) The man makes a type I error if his data provides enough evidence to show that the yogurt contains, on average, more than 3 grams of fat per serving, when in fact the yogurt does not.

b) The man makes a type II error if his data does not provide enough evidence to show that the yogurt contains, on average, more than 3 grams of fat per serving, when in fact the yogurt does.

c) There are 2 ways that a correct decision could be made. The man makes a correct decision if his data provides enough evidence to show that the yogurt contains, on average, more than 3 grams of fat per serving, when in fact the yogurt does. Or if his data does not provide enough evidence to show that the yogurt contains, on average, more than 3 grams of fat per serving, when in fact the yogurt does not.

Section 9.2

21) The significance level is the probability we will make a type I error if H_o is in fact true. We interpret it as the maximum risk we are willing to take of making a type I error.

22) The p-value is the chance of seeing a test statistic as inconsistent with the claimed mean as the one from our sample if H_o is in fact true. We interpret it as the actual risk we would be taking of making a type I error if we decide to reject H_o.

23) The test statistic is a value obtained from the sample that is used to determine whether or not we have enough evidence to reject H_o.

24) The more inconsistent the test statistic is with the claimed value of the mean, the more evidence we have against H_o.

25) When calculating the p-value for a two-tailed test, we must remember to double the area in the tail.

26) If the p-value is less than or equal to α, then we reject H_o because we feel that the risk of making a type I error is acceptable.

27) $\bar{x}$ is the sample mean. μ is the population mean. And μ_0 is the claimed mean.

28) False. In the long run, we will end up rejecting 10% of the true claims we test. Hopefully, we will reject far more than 10% of the false ones.

29) a) $z = \dfrac{42.66 - 41}{4.0524 \big/ \sqrt{35}} \approx 2.423$

b) $H_a : \mu > 41 \Rightarrow$ This is a right-tailed test.

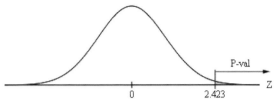

$P - val = normalcdf\left(2.423,\ 1*10^{99}\right)$

≈ 0.0077

c) $P - val \approx 0.0077 \le \alpha \Rightarrow$ Reject H_o
(Acceptable risk of a type I error)

31) a) $z = \dfrac{21.074 - 21.8}{3.005 \big/ \sqrt{40}} \approx -1.528$

b) $H_a : \mu \ne 21.8 \Rightarrow$ This is a two-tailed test.

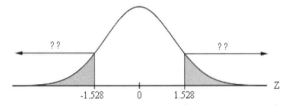

$P - val = 2 * normalcdf\left(1.528,\ 1*10^{99}\right)$

≈ 0.1265

Note: For a two-tailed test, it does not matter what side you find the area on (as long as you double the area.) Doubling before we round helps reduce rounding error.

c) $P - val \approx 0.1265 > \alpha \Rightarrow$
Do not Reject H_o (Risk of a type I error is too high)

33) a) $z = \dfrac{18.90 - 18.3}{0.8977 \big/ \sqrt{22}} \approx 3.135$

b) $H_a : \mu < 18.3 \Rightarrow$ This is a left-tailed test.

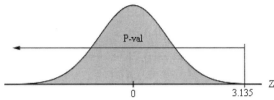

$P - val = normalcdf\left(-1*10^{99}, 3.135\right)$

≈ 0.9991

Note: Even though the z-score is on the right, this is a left-tailed test, so the P-val is the area to the left of the test statistic.

c) $P - val \approx 0.9991 > \alpha \Rightarrow$ Do not Reject H_o

35) Givens: The old value of the mean is \$6429, $\bar{x} = 7022$, and $n = 30$.

a) Step 1: The key word "Changed" does not indicate a specific direction.
$H_o : \mu = 6429$
$H_a : \mu \ne 6429$

Step 2: $\alpha = 0.05$

Step 3: $z = \dfrac{7022 - 6429}{1400 \big/ \sqrt{30}} \approx 2.320$

Step 4: $H_a : \mu \ne 6429 \Rightarrow$ This is a two-tailed test.

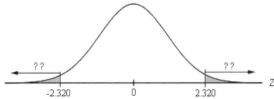

$P - val = 2 * normalcdf\left(2.320,\ 1*10^{99}\right)$

≈ 0.0203

Step 5: $P - val \approx 0.0203 \le \alpha \Rightarrow$ Reject H_o
(acceptable risk of making a type I error.)

Step 6: The data provides sufficient evidence, at the 5% significance level, to show that the ads are affecting sales.

b) Since $n = 30 \ge 30$, $\bar{x}$ will be normally distributed regardless of the distribution of the population. So, the requirements have been met.

37) Givens: Claimed mean is 3, $n = 18$

a) Step 1: The key phrase that the mean is "more" than 3 indicates:
$$H_o : \mu \le 3$$
$$H_a : \mu > 3$$

Step 2: $\alpha = 0.01$

Step 3: We are given that $\sigma = 0.29$ and from putting the data into the calculator we find that $\bar{x} \approx 3.06611$. So our test statistic is $z = \dfrac{3.06611 - 3}{0.29 / \sqrt{18}} \approx 0.967$

Note: To obtain accurate test statistics, it is often a good idea to round the mean beyond the minimum number of decimal places.

Step 4: $H_a : \mu > 3 \Rightarrow$ This is a right-tailed test.

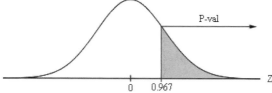

$P - val = normalcdf(0.967, 1 * 10^{99})$
≈ 0.1668

Step 5: $P - val \approx 0.1668 > \alpha \Rightarrow$ Do not reject H_o (too risky)

Step 6: The data did not provide enough evidence, at the 1% significance level, to show that the frozen yogurt contained, on average, more grams of fat per serving than claimed.

b) Since $15 \le n = 18 < 30$, we must hope that the population is not severely skewed.

c) No, in his sample, he did see more grams of fat per serving than claimed. However, the difference is small enough that it could just be caused by random variation of sample. He should start exercising.

d) Since we did not reject H_0, a type I error is not possible. However, if it turns out that H_0 is false, then we have made a type II error.

39) Givens: Nation mean is $3.097/gal., $n = 50$, and $\bar{x} = 3.465$.

a) Step 1: The key phrase "higher" than the national average indicates:
$$H_o : \mu \le 3.097$$
$$H_a : \mu > 3.097$$

Step 2: $\alpha = 0.05$

Step 3: We are given that $\sigma = 0.1425$, so we get $z = \dfrac{3.465 - 3.097}{0.1425 / \sqrt{50}} \approx 18.261$

Note: This large value for the test statistic often makes people fear that something is wrong. While this is a valid concern, we must remember that it may be the assumption that H_0 is true that is wrong. Such large values for the test statistic are great evidence against H_0.

Step 4: $H_a : \mu > 3.097 \Rightarrow$ This is a right-tailed test.

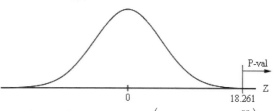

$P - val = normalcdf(18.261, 1 * 10^{99})$.
Entering this is the calculator we get:

```
normalcdf(18.261
,1*10^99)
      9.04556483E-75
```

The E-75 indicates that we must move the decimal 75 places to the left. Since we normally round P-values to 4 decimal places, we get . $P - val \approx 0.0000$

Step 5: $P - val \approx 0.0000 \le \alpha \Rightarrow$ Reject H_o (Acceptable risk of making a type I error)

Step 6: The data did provide enough evidence, at the 5% significance level, to show that California has, on average, higher prices than the nationwide average.

b) Since $n = 50 \ge 30$, $\bar{x}$ will be normally distributed regardless of the distribution of the population. The requirements have been met.

c) Because we rejected H_o, it is not possible that we have made a type II error, but it is possible that we have made a type I error. However, this seems extremely unlikely with a p-value of approx 0.0000. H_o would have to be true for a type I error to occur.

41) Givens: The old mean is 65.5 days, $n = 11$.
   a) Step 1: The key word "changed" indicates

$$H_o : \mu = 65.5$$

$$H_a : \mu \neq 65.5$$

Step 2: $\alpha = 0.05$

Step 3: We are given that $\sigma = 0.7925$ and from the calculator we get $\bar{x} \approx 65.69091$.

$$z = \frac{65.69091 - 65.5}{0.7925 / \sqrt{11}} \approx 0.799$$

Step 4: $H_a : \mu \neq 65.5 \Rightarrow$ This is a two-tailed test.

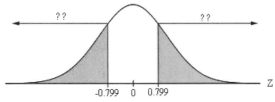

$P - val = 2 * normalcdf \left(0.799, \ 1 * 10^{99} \right)$

≈ 0.4243

Step 5: $P - val \approx 0.4243 > \alpha \Rightarrow$ Do Not Reject H_o (too risky)

Step 6: The data did not provide enough evidence, at the 5% significance level, to show that the average gestation time for house cats is different that it used to be.

b) Since $n = 11 < 15$, we must hope that house cat gestation times are normally distributed.

c) Since we did not reject H_o, it is not possible that we have made a type I error, but it is possible that we have made a type II error. H_o would have to be false for a type II error to have occurred.

43) Given: $n = 30$, $\bar{x} = 7022$, and $\sigma = 1400$.
   a) We need the z-scores for 95% confidence.

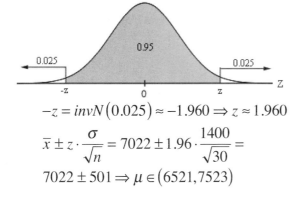

$-z = invN(0.025) \approx -1.960 \Rightarrow z \approx 1.960$

$$\bar{x} \pm z \cdot \frac{\sigma}{\sqrt{n}} = 7022 \pm 1.96 \cdot \frac{1400}{\sqrt{30}} =$$

$7022 \pm 501 \Rightarrow \mu \in (6521, 7523)$

b) We are 95% sure that the true mean sales lie somewhere in the interval. All the numbers in the interval are greater than, and therefore different from, 6429. Therefore, we should reject H_o. In symbols:

If $\mu \in (6521, 7523) \Rightarrow \mu \neq 6429$
$\Rightarrow H_o : \mu = 6429$ is false $\Rightarrow$ Reject H_o

45) Given: $n = 11$, $\bar{x} \approx 65.69$, and $\sigma = 0.7925$.
   a) We need the z-scores for 95% confidence.

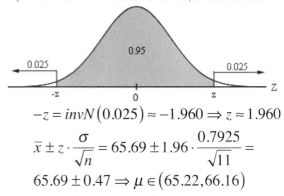

$-z = invN(0.025) \approx -1.960 \Rightarrow z \approx 1.960$

$$\bar{x} \pm z \cdot \frac{\sigma}{\sqrt{n}} = 65.69 \pm 1.96 \cdot \frac{0.7925}{\sqrt{11}} =$$

$65.69 \pm 0.47 \Rightarrow \mu \in (65.22, 66.16)$

b) If $\mu \in (65.22, 66.16) \Rightarrow \mu$ could be 65.5 $\Rightarrow$ $H_o : \mu = 65.5$ could be true $\Rightarrow$ Do not Reject H_o.

Section 9.3

47) We use t rather than z whenever σ is <u>unknown</u> and replaced by <u>s</u>.

48) Using t rather than z makes it <u>harder</u> to reject H_o.

49) a) Because σ is unknown, we must use s and, therefore, our test statistic is a t-score.

$$t = \frac{42.66 - 41}{4.4524 / \sqrt{22}} \approx 1.749$$

b) $H_a : \mu > 41 \Rightarrow$ This is a right-tailed test. Also, $df = n - 1 = 21$.

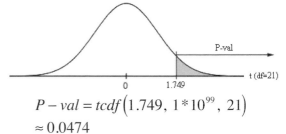

$P - val = tcdf \left(1.749, \ 1 * 10^{99}, \ 21 \right)$

≈ 0.0474

c) $P - val \approx 0.0474 \leq \alpha \Rightarrow$ Reject H_o (Acceptable risk of a type I error.)

51) a) Because σ is unknown, we must use s and, therefore, our test statistic is a t-score.

$$t = \frac{21.074 - 21.8}{2.805 / \sqrt{37}} \approx -1.574$$

b) $H_a : \mu \neq 21.8 \Rightarrow$ This is a two-tailed test. Also, $df = n - 1 = 36$.

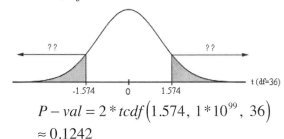

$$P - val = 2 * tcdf\left(1.574, 1*10^{99}, 36\right)$$
$$\approx 0.1242$$

c) $P - val \approx 0.1242 > \alpha \Rightarrow$ Do not Reject H_o (Too Risky)

53) a) Because σ is unknown, we must use s and, therefore, our test statistic is a t-score.

$$t = \frac{18.90 - 18.3}{0.8557 / \sqrt{42}} \approx 4.544$$

b) $H_a : \mu < 18.3 \Rightarrow$ This is a left-tailed test. Also, $df = n - 1 = 41$.

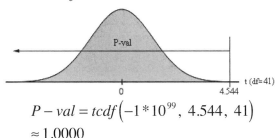

$$P - val = tcdf\left(-1*10^{99}, 4.544, 41\right)$$
$$\approx 1.0000$$

c) $P - val \approx 1.0000 > \alpha \Rightarrow$ Do not Reject H_o (Too Risky)

55) Givens: Claimed mean is 22 mpg, $n = 16$, $\bar{x} = 21.6$, $s = 0.948$.

a) Step 1: We want to show the mean is "less than" claimed, so we get: $\begin{array}{l} H_o : \mu \geq 22 \\ H_a : \mu < 22 \end{array}$

Step 2: $\alpha = 0.01$

Step 3: Because σ is unknown, we must use s and, therefore, our test statistic is a t-score. $t = \dfrac{21.6 - 22}{0.948 / \sqrt{16}} \approx -1.688$

Step 4: $H_a : \mu < 22 \Rightarrow$ This is a left-tailed test. Also, $df = n - 1 = 15$.

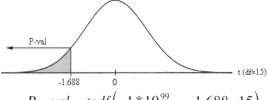

$$P - val = tcdf\left(-1*10^{99}, -1.688, 15\right)$$
$$\approx 0.0560$$

Step 5: $P - val \approx 0.0560 > \alpha \Rightarrow$ Do Not Reject H_o (Too Risky)

Step 6: The data does not provide enough evidence, at the 1% significance level, to show that the average highway mileage for all the trucks is less than 22 mpg.

b) Since $15 \leq n = 16 < 30$, we must hope that the population is not severely skewed.

57) Givens: The claimed mean is 3 grams, $n = 18$.

a) Step 1: We want to see if the average is "more grams" than claimed. So, $\begin{array}{l} H_o : \mu \leq 3 \\ H_a : \mu > 3 \end{array}$

Step 2: $\alpha = 0.01$

Step 3: No mean or standard deviation is given, so we will use STAT > CALC > 1-Var Stats to find them. Since we are entering sample data, we must report sample values. $\bar{x} \approx 3.06611$; $s \approx 0.19309$
Because σ is unknown, we are using s and, therefore, our test statistic is a t-score.

$$t = \frac{3.06611 - 3}{0.19309 / \sqrt{18}} \approx 1.453$$

Step 4: $H_a : \mu > 3 \Rightarrow$ This is a right-tailed test. Also, $df = n - 1 = 17$.

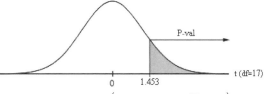

$$P - val = tcdf\left(1.453, 1*10^{99}, 17\right)$$
$$\approx 0.0822$$

Step 5: $P - val \approx 0.0822 > \alpha \Rightarrow$ Do Not Reject H_o (Too Risky)

Step 6: The data does not provide enough evidence, at the 1% significance level, to show that the yogurt contains, on average, more than 3 grams of fat per serving.

b)   Since $15 \leq n = 18 < 30$, we must hope that the population is not severely skewed.

c)   No, there is not enough evidence to prove that there is more fat than claimed.

59) Givens: The old mean was $6429, $n = 30$, $\overline{x} = 7022$, $s = 1336$.

a)   Step 1: The key phrase "affecting" sales,
$$H_o : \mu = 6429$$
does not indicate a direction.
$$H_a : \mu \neq 6429$$

Step 2: $\alpha = 0.05$
Step 3: Because σ is unknown, we must use s and, therefore, our test statistic is a t-score. $t = \dfrac{7022 - 6426}{1336 / \sqrt{30}} \approx 2.431$

Step 4: $H_a : \mu \neq 6429 \Rightarrow$ This is a two-tailed test. Also, $df = n - 1 = 29$.

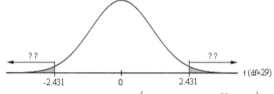

$$P - val = 2 * tcdf\left(2.431, 1*10^{99}, 29\right)$$
$$\approx 0.0215$$

Step 5: $P - val \approx 0.0215 \leq \alpha \Rightarrow$ Reject H_o (Acceptable risk of making a type I error)
Step 6: The data provides enough evidence, at the 5% significance level, to show that the ads are affecting sales.

b)   Since $n = 30 \geq 30$, we know that $\overline{x}$ is normally distributed and the requirements have been met.

c)   Since we rejected H_0, it not possible that we have made a type II error. However, if H_0 turns out to be true, then we have made a type I error. We perceive the risk of this to be about 2.15%.

61) Givens: The old mean was 11 hours, $n = 30$.

a)   Step 1: The want to see if the change has "shortened" the lasting time .
$$H_o : \mu \geq 11$$
$$H_a : \mu < 11$$

Step 2: $\alpha = 0.10$
Step 3: No mean or standard deviation is given, so we will use STAT > CALC > 1-Var Stats to find them. Since we are entering sample data, we must report sample values.
$\overline{x} = 10.428$; $s \approx 1.2903$
Because σ is unknown, we are using s and, therefore, our test statistic is a t-score.

$$t = \dfrac{10.428 - 11}{1.2903 / \sqrt{30}} \approx -2.428$$

Step 4: $H_a : \mu < 11 \Rightarrow$ This is a left-tailed test. Also, $df = n - 1 = 29$.

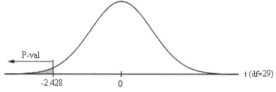

$$P - val = tcdf\left(-1 * 10^{99}, -2.428, 29\right)$$
$$\approx 0.0108$$

Step 5: $P - val \approx 0.0108 \leq \alpha \Rightarrow$ Reject H_o (Acceptable risk of making a type I error)
Step 6: The data did provide enough evidence, at the 10% significance level, to show that the average effectiveness time has been decreased.

b)   Since $n = 30 \geq 30$, $\overline{x}$ will be normally distributed regardless of the distribution of the population. So the requirements have been met.

c)   Not really. Even though we are convinced that the average effectiveness time is less than 11 hours, it probably is not too much lower. The true mean must be nearer to the sample mean of 10.428 hours than the value of 11 hours which we rejected.

d) $\mu = 10.8 \Rightarrow H_o : \mu \geq 11$ is false. In step 5 we rejected H_o. Rejecting a false claim is a correct decision.

63) Givens: Comparable mean is \$3.097/gallon,
$n = 50$, $\bar{x} = 3.465$, $s = 0.176$.

a) Step 1: We want to see if the average price
is "higher" in CA.
$$H_o : \mu \le 3.097$$
$$H_a : \mu > 3.097$$

Step 2: $\alpha = 0.05$

Step 3: Because σ is unknown, we must use
s and, therefore, our test statistic is a t-
score. $t = \dfrac{3.465 - 3.097}{0.176 / \sqrt{50}} \approx 14.785$

Step 4: $H_a : \mu > 3.097 \Rightarrow$ This is a right-
tailed test. Also, $df = n - 1 = 49$.

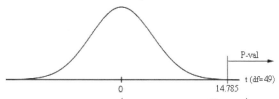

$$P - val = tcdf\left(14.785,\ 1*10^{99},\ 49\right)$$

Entering this in the calculator produces:

```
tcdf(14.785,1*10
^99,49)
       5.39722157E-20
```

The E-20 indicates that we must move the
decimal 20 places to the left. Since we
normally round P-values to 4 decimal
places, we get . $P - val \approx 0.0000$

Step 5: $P - val \approx 0.0000 \le \alpha \Rightarrow$ Reject H_o
(Acceptable risk of making a type I error)

Step 6: The data did provide enough
evidence, at the 5% significance level, to
show that California pays, on average,
higher prices than the nationwide
average.

b) Since $n = 50 \ge 30$, $\bar{x}$ will be normally
distributed regardless of the distribution of
the population. So the requirements have
been met.

c) $\mu = 3.42 \Rightarrow H_o : \mu \le 3.097$ is false. In
step 5 we rejected H_o. Rejecting a false
claim is a correct decision.

65) Givens: $n = 16$, $\bar{x} = 21.6$, $s = 0.948$.

a) We need the t-scores for 98% confidence
with $df = n - 1 = 15$.

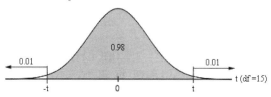

From the t-table we find $t_{0.01} = 2.602$.
$$\bar{x} \pm t \cdot \frac{s}{\sqrt{n}} = 21.6 \pm 2.602 \cdot \frac{0.948}{\sqrt{16}} =$$
$$21.6 \pm 0.6 \Rightarrow \mu \in (21.0,\ 22.2)$$

b) We are 98% confident that the true
population mean for the trucks is
somewhere between 21.0 and 22.2 mpg. This
means that it could be 22 mpg. If it is
possible that the mean really is 22 mpg,
then we should not reject the manufacturer's
claim that it is 22 mpg. This was the
decision we reached on problem 55.

In symbols: If $\mu \in (21.0, 22.2) \Rightarrow \mu$ could
be $22 \Rightarrow H_o : u \ge 22$ could be true $\Rightarrow$ Do Not
Reject H_o

67) Givens: $n = 50$, $\bar{x} = 3.465$, $s = 0.176$

a) We need the t-scores for 90% confidence
with $df = n - 1 = 49$. However, there is
no $df = 49$ line on the t-table, so we will
round down and use $df = 45$.

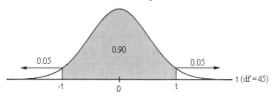

From the t-table we find $t_{0.05} = 1.679$.
$$\bar{x} \pm t \cdot \frac{s}{\sqrt{n}} = 3.465 \pm 1.679 \cdot \frac{0.176}{\sqrt{50}} =$$
$$3.465 \pm 0.042 \Rightarrow \mu \in (3.423,\ 3.507)$$

b) $\mu \in (3.423, 3.507) \Rightarrow \mu > 3.097 \Rightarrow$
$H_o : \mu \le 3.097$ is false $\Rightarrow$ Do Not Reject
H_o. This agrees with our decision from (63)

Section 9.4

69) $\hat{p}$ is the symbol for the <u>sample</u> proportion. p is the symbol for the <u>population</u> proportion. p_0 is the symbol for the <u>claimed</u> proportion.

70) We use p when we are working with proportions, but we also use it for <u>percentages</u> & <u>probabilities</u>.

71) In a proportion test, evidence consists of a large <u>difference</u> between $\hat{p}$ and p_0.

72) In general, evidence in a hypothesis test comes from seeing large differences between what we observed in the <u>sample</u> and what we expected to see if H_o was <u>true</u> .

73) a) $\hat{p} = \dfrac{x}{n} = \dfrac{446}{768} \approx 0.5807 \Rightarrow$

$z = \dfrac{0.5807 - 0.63}{\sqrt{\dfrac{0.63 * 0.37}{768}}} \approx -2.830$

b) $H_a : p > 0.63 \Rightarrow$ This is a left-tailed test.

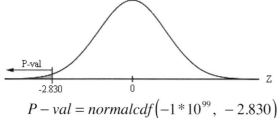

$P - val = normalcdf\left(-1 * 10^{99},\ -2.830\right)$

≈ 0.0023

c) $P - val \approx 0.0023 \leq \alpha \Rightarrow$ Reject H_o
(Acceptable risk of making a type I error)

75) a) $z = \dfrac{0.061 - 0.084}{\sqrt{\dfrac{0.084 * 0.916}{255}}} \approx -1.324$

b) $H_a : p \neq 0.084 \Rightarrow$ This is a two-tailed test.

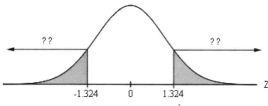

$P - val = 2 * normalcdf\left(1.324,\ 1 * 10^{99}\right)$

≈ 0.1855

c) $P - val \approx 0.1855 > \alpha \Rightarrow$ Do Not Reject H_o
(Risk of a type I error is too high)

77) Givens: Claimed proportion is 0.17, $n = 218$, $x = 19$

a)   Step 1: We want to see if the percentage has "decreased" since 1985.
$$H_o : p \geq 0.17$$
$$H_a : p < 0.17$$

Step 2: $\alpha = 0.05$

Step 3: $\hat{p} = \dfrac{x}{n} = \dfrac{19}{218} \approx 0.0872 \Rightarrow$

$z = \dfrac{0.0872 - 0.17}{\sqrt{\dfrac{0.17 * 0.83}{218}}} \approx -3.255$

Step 4: $H_a : p < 0.17 \Rightarrow$ This is a left-tailed test.

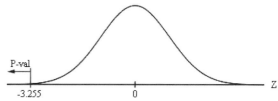

$P - val = normalcdf\left(-1 * 10^{99},\ -3.255\right)$

≈ 0.0006

Step 5: $P - val \approx 0.0006 \leq \alpha \Rightarrow$ Reject H_o
(Acceptable risk of making a type I error)
Step 6: The data provided enough evidence, at the 5% significance level, to show that the percentage of the current workforce that uses drugs during a given one month period has decreased from the 1985 percentage.

b)   Since we rejected the null hypothesis, it is not possible that we have made a type II error.

c) $np_o = 218(0.17) = 37.06 \geq 5$
$nq_o = 218(0.83) = 180.94 \geq 5$
$\Rightarrow$ the requirements have been met

79) Givens: $n = 493$, $\hat{p} = 0.507$

a)   Step 1: A "majority" means more than half or greater than 0.5.
$$H_o : p \leq 0.5$$
$$H_a : p > 0.5$$

Step 2: $\alpha = 0.10$

Step 3: $z = \dfrac{0.507 - 0.50}{\sqrt{\dfrac{0.50 * 0.50}{493}}} \approx 0.311$

Step 4: $H_a : p > 0.50 \Rightarrow$ This is a right-tailed test.

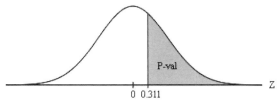

$$P - val = normalcdf\left(0.311, \, 1*10^{99}\right)$$

$$\approx 0.3779$$

Step 5: $P - val \approx 0.3779 > \alpha \Rightarrow$ Do Not Reject H_o (Too Risky)

Step 6: The data does not provide enough evidence, at the 10% significance level, to show that the candidate will win without a run-off election.

b) Since we did not reject the null hypothesis, it is not possible that we have made a type I error.

c) $np_o = 493(0.5) = 246.5 \geq 5$

$nq_o = 493(0.5) = 246.5 \geq 5$

$\Rightarrow$ the requirements have been met

81) Givens: Comparable proportion is 0.47, $n = 314$, $x = 239$

a) Step 1: We want to show that the proportion is "higher" in the bay area.

$H_o : p \leq 0.47$

$H_a : p > 0.47$

Step 2: $\alpha = 0.01$

Step 3: $\hat{p} = \dfrac{x}{n} = \dfrac{239}{314} \approx 0.7611 \Rightarrow$

$$z = \dfrac{0.7611 - 0.47}{\sqrt{\dfrac{0.47 * 0.53}{314}}} \approx 10.335$$

Step 4: $H_a : p > 0.47 \Rightarrow$ This is a right-tailed test.

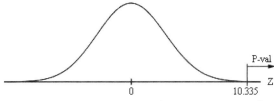

$$P - val = normalcdf\left(10.335, \, 1*10^{99}\right)$$

Entering this in the calculator, we get:

```
normalcdf(10.335
,1*10^99)
      2.49976914E-25
```

The $E\text{-}25$ indicates that we must move the decimal 25 places to the left. Since we normally round P-values to 4 decimal places, we get . $P - val \approx 0.0000$

Step 5: $P - val \approx 0.0000 \leq \alpha \Rightarrow$ Reject H_o (Acceptable risk of making a type I error)

Step 6: The data does provide enough evidence, at the 1% significance level, to show that the proportion of people with high-speed internet access at home is higher than for the nation as a whole.

b) $np_o = 314(0.47) = 147.58 \geq 5$

$nq_o = 314(0.53) = 166.42 \geq 5$

$\Rightarrow$ the requirements have been met.

c) $p = 0.68 \Rightarrow H_o : p \leq 0.47$ is false $\Rightarrow$ Rejecting H_o was a correct decision.

83) Givens: $n = 450$, $x = 60$. No value for p seems to be claimed, but if the die is fair, then the number 4 would show up $1/6$ of the time or approximately 16.67% of the time.

Step 1: The phrases "not fair" and not showing up the "proper proportion" of times do not indicate a direction. So, we get

$H_o : p = 0.1667$

$H_a : p \neq 0.1667$

Step 2: $\alpha = 0.10$

Step 3: $\hat{p} = \dfrac{x}{n} = \dfrac{60}{450} \approx 0.1333 \Rightarrow$

$$z = \dfrac{0.1333 - 0.1667}{\sqrt{\dfrac{0.1667 * 0.8333}{450}}} \approx -1.901$$

Step 4: $H_a : p \neq 0.1667 \Rightarrow$ This is a two-tailed test.

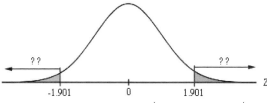

$$P - val = 2 * normalcdf\left(1.901, \, 1*10^{99}\right)$$

$$\approx 0.0573$$

Step 5: $P - val \approx 0.0573 \leq \alpha \Rightarrow$ Reject H_o (Acceptable risk of making a type I error)

Step 6: The data provided enough evidence, at the 10% significance level, to show that the die is not fair.

85) Givens: The comparable proportion is 0.527, $n = 73$, $x = 10$

   a) Step 1: We are trying to show that the events are dependent. This would mean that

$$P(\text{passing}|\text{computer projects}) \neq P(\text{passing})$$

$$\Rightarrow p \neq 0.527 \Rightarrow \begin{array}{l} H_o : p = 0.527 \\ H_a : p \neq 0.527 \end{array}$$

Step 2: $\alpha = 0.10$

Step 3: $\hat{p} = \dfrac{x}{n} = \dfrac{10}{73} \approx 0.1370 \Rightarrow$

$$z = \frac{0.1370 - 0.527}{\sqrt{\dfrac{0.527 * 0.473}{73}}} \approx -6.674$$

Step 4: $H_a : p \neq 0.527 \Rightarrow$ This is a two-tailed test.

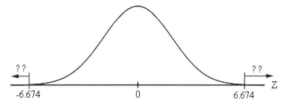

$$P - val = 2 * normalcdf\left(6.674,\ 1*10^{99}\right)$$
$$\approx 0.0000$$

Step 5: $P - val \approx 0.0000 \leq \alpha \Rightarrow$ Reject H_o (Acceptable risk of making a type I error)

Step 6: The data provided more than enough evidence, at the 10% significance level, to show that passing the class is dependent on doing the computer projects.

   b) The passing rate in the sample of students who did not do their computer projects was much lower than the standard passing rate. Therefore, I conclude that students who do not do their computer projects have a much lower chance of passing the course.

87) Givens: $n = 493$, $\hat{p} = 0.507$

   a) We need the z-scores for 80% confidence.

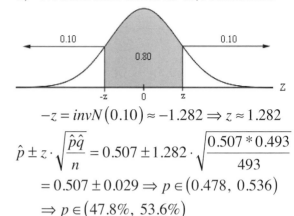

$$-z = invN(0.10) \approx -1.282 \Rightarrow z \approx 1.282$$

$$\hat{p} \pm z \cdot \sqrt{\frac{\hat{p}\hat{q}}{n}} = 0.507 \pm 1.282 \cdot \sqrt{\frac{0.507 * 0.493}{493}}$$

$$= 0.507 \pm 0.029 \Rightarrow p \in (0.478,\ 0.536)$$

$$\Rightarrow p \in (47.8\%,\ 53.6\%)$$

   b) We are 80% confident that the percentage of likely voters that will vote for the candidate in question is somewhere between 47.8% and 53.6%. Therefore, it is possible that the candidate will receive less than 50% of the vote. So, we should not reject $H_o : p \leq 0.5$.

In symbols:
If $p \in (0.478, 0.536) \Rightarrow p$ could be 0.50
$\Rightarrow H_o : p \leq 0.5$ could be true
$\Rightarrow$ do not reject H_o

89) Givens: $n = 314$, $x = 239$,

$$\hat{p} = \frac{x}{n} = \frac{239}{314} \approx 0.7611$$

   a) We need the z-scores for 98% confidence.

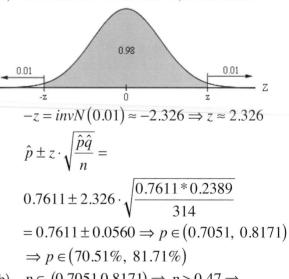

$$-z = invN(0.01) \approx -2.326 \Rightarrow z \approx 2.326$$

$$\hat{p} \pm z \cdot \sqrt{\frac{\hat{p}\hat{q}}{n}} =$$

$$0.7611 \pm 2.326 \cdot \sqrt{\frac{0.7611 * 0.2389}{314}}$$

$$= 0.7611 \pm 0.0560 \Rightarrow p \in (0.7051,\ 0.8171)$$

$$\Rightarrow p \in (70.51\%,\ 81.71\%)$$

   b) $p \in (0.7051, 0.8171) \Rightarrow p > 0.47 \Rightarrow$ $H_o : p \leq 0.47$ is false $\Rightarrow$ We should reject H_o.

Chapter Problem:

a) Givens: $\mu = 27.1$, $\alpha = 0.20$, $H_0 : \mu \geq 27.6$, $H_a : \mu < 27.6$, $\sigma = 4.519$, $n = 37$

Step 1: Find the z value that would have a P-value of 0.20 for a left-tailed test.

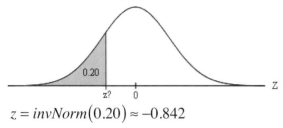

$z = invNorm(0.20) \approx -0.842$

Step 2: Convert this z value to an $\overline{x}$.

$\overline{x} = \mu_0 - 0.842\sigma_{\overline{x}} \approx 27.6 - 0.842 \cdot \dfrac{4.519}{\sqrt{37}}$

≈ 26.9745

Step 3: Determine $P(\overline{x} \leq 26.9745 | \mu = 27.1)$.

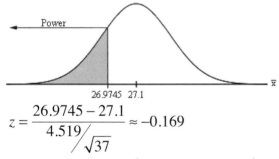

$z = \dfrac{26.9745 - 27.1}{4.519 / \sqrt{37}} \approx -0.169$

$Power = normalcdf(-1*10^{99}, -0.169)$

≈ 0.4329

b) A higher significance level means we are willing to take a higher risk of making a type I error. This will cause us to reject claims more often. This will result in us rejecting more false claims.

Section 10.1

1) Total area under the curve is 1; height approaches zero on the right; when df is large chi-square curve is roughly bell shaped.

3) a) df of 10 is just to the right of the high point.

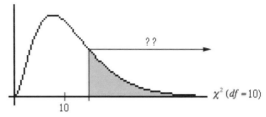

b) $\chi^2 cdf(14.76, 1*10^{99}, 10) \approx 0.1411$

5) a) df of 17 is just to the right of the high point.

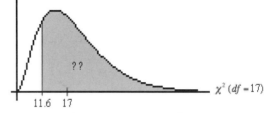

b) $\chi^2 cdf(11.6, 1*10^{99}, 17) \approx 0.8237$

7) a) df of 15 is just to the right of the high point.

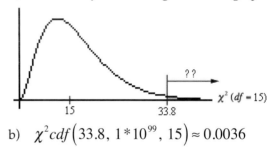

b) $\chi^2 cdf(33.8, 1*10^{99}, 15) \approx 0.0036$

Section 10.2

9) When calculating the test statistic for a Goodness-of-fit test, the 'O' stands for the observed frequency and the values of 'O' are obtained from the sample.

10) When calculating the test statistics for a goodness-of-fit test, the 'E' stands for the expected frequency. These are the frequencies we expect to see if H_o is true.

11) The degrees of freedom for a goodness-of-fit test is given by the formula $df = k - 1$, where the k stands for the number of categories.

12) The values of $\dfrac{(O-E)^2}{E}$ can be thought of as mini z-scores. The larger these values get, the more evidence we have against H_o.

13) We must always have the possibility of equality in H_o so that we know what frequencies to expect if H_o true. A phrase like 'equals' tells us what to expect. A phrase like 'not equal' tells us what NOT to expect.

14) We would need to explain to them that we can not prove that the distribution is the same, but we can try to prove that it is different. If we fail to prove it is different, then it is a reasonable possibility that the distribution is the same, but it remains uncertain.

15) a) Step 1:

H_o: the success rates for student athletes are the same as those of all the students

H_a: the success rates for student athletes are different from those of all the students

Step 2: $\alpha = 0.01$

Step 3: We need to make a table to get the test statistic. The observed frequencies, O, are from the sample. The values of p, are given.

Grade	O	p_i	$E = np_i$	$\dfrac{(O-E)^2}{E}$
Pass	43	0.665	40.565	0.146
Not P	10	0.120	7.32	0.981
W	8	0.215	13.115	1.995
	61	1.000	61	3.122

$$\chi^2 = \sum \frac{(O-E)^2}{E} \approx 3.122$$

Step 4: $df = k - 1 = 3 - 1 = 2$

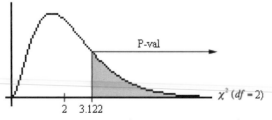

$$P - val \approx \chi^2 cdf\left(3.122, 1*10^{99}, 2\right)$$
$$\approx 0.2099$$

Step 5: $P - val \approx 0.2099 > \alpha \Rightarrow$ Do Not Reject H_o (Too Risky)

Step 6: There is not enough evidence, at the 1% significance level, to show that the success rates for student athletes are different from those of all the students.

b) All expected frequencies ≥ 5, so the requirements have been met.

17) a) Step 1:

H_o: the ethnic breakdown in Livermore is the same as the ethnic breakdown in Hayward.

H_a: the ethnic breakdown in Livermore is different than the ethnic breakdown in Hayward

Step 2: $\alpha = 0.05$

Step 3: The values of O are from the sample, and we convert the given percentages to decimals to get p.

Ethn	O	p_i	$E = np_i$	$\dfrac{(O-E)^2}{E}$
White	209	0.511	127.75	51.676
Black	4	0.094	23.5	16.181
Asian	11	0.146	36.5	17.815
Hispa	25	0.240	60	20.417
Other	1	0.009	2.25	0.694
	250	1.000	250	106.783

$$\chi^2 = \sum \frac{(O-E)^2}{E} \approx 106.783$$

Step 4: $df = k - 1 = 5 - 1 = 4$

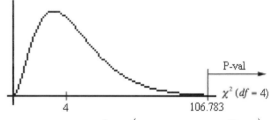

$$P - val \approx \chi^2 cdf\left(106.783, 1*10^{99}, 4\right)$$
$$\approx 0.0000$$

Step 5: $P - val \approx 0.0000 \leq \alpha \Rightarrow$ Reject H_o (Acceptable risk of making a type I error)

Step 6: There is enough evidence, at the 5% significance level, to show that the ethnic breakdown in Livermore is different than the ethnic breakdown in Hayward.

b) 80% of the E's (4 out of 5) are at least 5 and all of them are at least 1, so the requirements have been met.

c) We Rejected H_o so it is possible that we have made a type I error. This will be the case if H_o turns out to be true. However, our P-value was extremely low which means that there is not much risk that we have made a type I error. We can be confident in our decision.

d) Because we Rejected H_o, it is NOT possible that we have made a type II error.

19) a) Step 1:

H_o: the distribution of the use of hands-free devices did not change after the law went into effect.

H_a: the distribution of the use of hands-free devices changed after the law went into effect.

Step 2: $\alpha = 0.01$

Step 3: The values of O are from the sample, and we convert the given percentages to decimals to get p.

Answer	O	p_i	$E = np_i$	$\dfrac{(O-E)^2}{E}$
Always	158	0.481	249.158	33.351
Some	170	0.306	158.508	0.833
Never	190	0.213	110.334	57.522
	518	1.000	518	91.706

$$\chi^2 = \sum \frac{(O-E)^2}{E} \approx 91.706$$

Step 4: $df = k - 1 = 3 - 1 = 2$

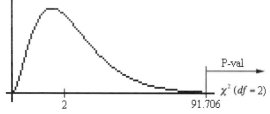

$$P - val \approx \chi^2 cdf\left(91.706, 1*10^{99}, 2\right)$$

≈ 0.0000

Step 5: $P - val \approx 0.0000 \leq \alpha \Rightarrow$ Reject H_o (Acceptable risk of making a type I error)

Step 6: There is enough evidence, at the 1% significance level, to show that the distribution of the use of hands-free devices changed after the law went into effect.

b) 100% of the E's are at least 5, so the requirements have been met.

c) Never provided the most evidence against H_o (its $\dfrac{(O-E)^2}{E}$ provides the biggest contribution to the test stat)

d) Sometimes provided the least evidence against H_o (its $\dfrac{(O-E)^2}{E}$ provides the smallest contribution to the test stat)

21) a) Step 1:

H_o: the die is fair.

H_a: the die is not fair.

Step 2: $\alpha = 0.01$

Step 3: The values of O are from the sample. The values of p are not given. However, if the die is fair, then each number would have a 1/6 chance of occurring.

Number	O	p_i	$E = np_i$	$\dfrac{(O-E)^2}{E}$
1	30	1/6	25	1.00
2	22	1/6	25	0.36
3	12	1/6	25	6.76
4	28	1/6	25	0.36
5	23	1/6	25	0.16
6	35	1/6	25	4.00
	150	1	150	12.64

$$\chi^2 = \sum \frac{(O-E)^2}{E} = 12.64$$

Step 4: $df = k - 1 = 6 - 1 = 5$

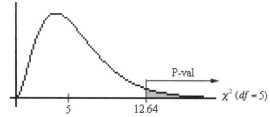

$$P - val \approx \chi^2 cdf\left(12.64, 1*10^{99}, 5\right)$$

≈ 0.0270

Step 5: $P - val \approx 0.0270 > \alpha \Rightarrow$ Do Not Reject H_o (Too risky)

Step 6: There is not enough evidence, at the 1% significance level, to show that the die is not fair.

b) Yes, because if we had Rejected H_o, there would only have been a 2.7% risk that we were making a type I error. That means, there is a good chance that the die is not fair, just not enough evidence to prove our case at the 1% significance level.

c) Only if H_o is False. If H_o is true, then we have a 1% chance of rejecting it and making a type I error regardless of our sample size.

23) a) Step 1:
H_o: the population distribution of flavors of all the candies is evenly distributed.
H_a: the population distribution of flavors of all the candies is not evenly distributed.
Step 2: $\alpha = 0.10$
Step 3: The values of O are from the sample. The values of p are not given. However, if the flavors are all evenly distributed, then each flavor would have a $1/4$ chance of occurring.

Flavor	O	p_i	$E = np_i$	$\dfrac{(O-E)^2}{E}$
cherry	15	1/4	10.5	1.929
lemon	7	1/4	10.5	1.167
orange	9	1/4	10.5	0.214
straw	11	1/4	10.5	0.024
	42	1	42	3.334

$$\chi^2 = \sum \frac{(O-E)^2}{E} \approx 3.334$$

Step 4: $df = k - 1 = 4 - 1 = 3$

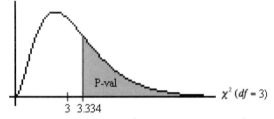

$$P - val \approx \chi^2 cdf\left(3.334, 1*10^{99}, 3\right)$$
$$\approx 0.3429$$

Step 5: $P - val \approx 0.3429 > \alpha \Rightarrow$ Do Not Reject H_o (Too risky)

Step 6: There is not enough evidence, at the 10% significance level, to show that the population distribution of flavors of all the candies is not evenly distributed.

b) A type I error would have occurred if we had enough evidence to show that the population distribution of flavors of all the candies is not evenly distributed, when in fact it is evenly distributed.

c) A type II error would have occurred if we did not have enough evidence to show that the population distribution of flavors of all the candies is not evenly distributed, when in fact it is not evenly distributed.

<u>Section 10.3</u>

25) For a chi-square test of independence, the degrees of freedom is given by the formula $df = (r-1)(c-1)$, where r is the number of <u>row</u> categories and c is the number of <u>column</u> categories.

26) In the test statistic for a chi-square test of independence, the 'E' stands for the frequency we expect if H_o is <u>true</u>. This means that it is calculated under the assumption that the variables in question are <u>independent</u>.

27) H_o must include equality and if two variable are independent, then certain formulas are equal, whereas if they are dependent those formulas are not equal. Thus big differences in these formulas will then provide strong evidence against H_o.

28) We must explain to them that hypothesis tests can not prove independence, but we can try to prove that they are dependent. If we fail to prove they are dependent, then independence will be left as a reasonable possibility.

29) a) Step 1:

H_o: the players performance is independent of the number of runners on base at the time of the at bat.

H_a: the players performance is dependent on the number of runners on base at the time of the at bat.

Step 2: $\alpha = 0.10$

Step 3: Calculate the expected frequencies for each cell using the formula: $E = \dfrac{R \cdot C}{n}$.

Number of runners on base

	0	1	2	3	Totals
Out	157	128	87	10	382
	152.93	129.96	87.95	11.16	
Single	57	50	20	4	131
	52.45	44.57	30.16	3.83	
Extra Bases	19	20	27	3	69
	27.62	23.47	15.89	2.02	
Totals	233	198	134	17	582

$$\chi^2 = \sum \frac{(O-E)^2}{E}$$

$$\approx 0.108 + 0.030 + 0.010 + 0.121$$
$$+ 0.395 + 0.662 + 3.423 + 0.008$$
$$+ 2.690 + 0.513 + 7.768 + 0.475$$
$$= 16.203$$

Step 4: $df = (r-1)(c-1) = 2*3 = 6$

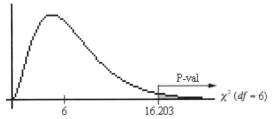

$$P - val \approx \chi^2 cdf\left(16.203, 1*10^{99}, 6\right)$$
$$\approx 0.0127$$

Step 5: $P - val \approx 0.0127 \leq \alpha \Rightarrow$ Reject H_o (Acceptable risk of making a type I error)

Step 6: There is enough evidence, at the 10% significance level, to show that the players performance is dependent on the number of runners on base at the time of the at bat.

b) All expected frequencies were at least 1 and only 10/12 or 83.3%% of the cells had expected frequencies ≥ 5. Since this is at least 80%, the requirements have been satisfied.

c) Even though we were able to reject, the biggest reason was because the player had many more extra base hits when there were 2 runners on base. Since this represents an area of strong performance, the fans can't really back up their claim.

31) a) Step 1:

H_o: American's priority between creating additional energy sources is independent of their political affiliation.

H_a: American's priority between creating additional energy sources is dependent on their political affiliation.

Step 2: $\alpha = 0.05$

Step 3: Calculate the expected frequencies for each cell using the formula: $E = \dfrac{R \cdot C}{n}$.

Which takes priority?

	Energy	Environ	Don't Know	Totals
Repub	261	228	55	544
	208.03	277.52	58.45	
Democ	148	297	51	496
	189.67	253.04	53.29	
Indep	43	78	21	142
	54.30	72.44	15.26	
Totals	452	603	127	1,182

$$\chi^2 = \sum \frac{(O-E)^2}{E}$$

$$\approx 13.488 + 8.836 + 0.204$$
$$+ 9.155 + 7.637 + 0.098$$
$$+ 2.352 + 0.427 + 2.159$$
$$= 44.356$$

Step 4: $df = (r-1)(c-1) = 2*2 = 4$

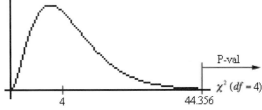

$$P - val \approx \chi^2 cdf\left(44.356, 1*10^{99}, 4\right)$$
$$\approx 0.0000$$

Step 5: $P - val \approx 0.0000 \leq \alpha \Rightarrow$ Reject H_o (Acceptable risk of making a type I error)

Step 6: There is enough evidence, at the 5% significance level, to show that American's priority between creating additional energy sources is dependent on their political affiliation.

b) Most evidence was from the Repub/Energy cell, because it contributed the largest amount to the test stat. The least was from the Democ/Don't know cell, because it contributed the smallest amount to the test statistic.

c) Highest percentage for Energy as the top priority was for Republicans at 48.0%. Highest percentage for the Environment as the top priority was for Democrats at 59.9%.

d) $E = n \cdot p = n \cdot P(\text{Repub \& Energy})$
$= n \cdot P(\text{Repub}) \cdot P(\text{Energy})$
$\approx 1182 \cdot \dfrac{544}{1182} \cdot \dfrac{452}{1182} = \dfrac{544 \cdot 452}{1182}$
≈ 208.03

33) a) Step 1: H_o: the level of coffee drinking of Chabot students is independent of the season in which they were born.
H_a: the level of coffee drinking of Chabot students is dependent on the season in which they were born.
Step 2: $\alpha = 0.10$
Step 3: Calculate the expected frequencies for each cell using the formula: $E = \dfrac{R \cdot C}{n}$.

How often do you drink coffee?

	Daily	Sometimes	Never	Totals
Autumn	4 4.60	10 9.66	6 5.75	20
Winter	8 5.52	12 11.59	4 6.90	24
Spring	5 5.75	11 12.07	9 7.18	25
Summer	3 4.14	9 8.69	6 5.17	18
Totals	20	42	25	87

$\chi^2 = \sum \dfrac{(O-E)^2}{E}$
$\approx 0.078 + 0.012 + 0.011$
$+ 1.114 + 0.015 + 1.219$
$+ 0.098 + 0.095 + 0.461$
$+ 0.314 + 0.011 + 0.133$
$= 3.561$

Step 4: $df = (r-1)(c-1) = 3*2 = 6$

$P - val \approx \chi^2 cdf\left(3.561, 1*10^{99}, 6\right)$
≈ 0.7358

Step 5: $P - val \approx 0.7358 > \alpha \Rightarrow$ Do Not Reject H_o (Too risky)

Step 6: There is not enough evidence, at the 10% significance level, to show that the level of coffee drinking of Chabot students is dependent on the season in which they were born.

b) All expected frequencies were at least 1 and only 10/12 or 83.3%% of the cells had expected frequencies ≥ 5. Since this is at least 80%, the requirements have been satisfied.

c) Since we did not reject H_o, it is possible that we have made a type II error. This will be the case if it turns out that H_o is false.

35) a) Step 1:
H_o: the number of accidents in the last 3 years is independent of the age of the student.
H_a: the number of accidents in the last 3 years is dependent on the age of the student.
Step 2: $\alpha = 0.05$

Step 3: Calculate E's using: $E = \dfrac{R \cdot C}{n}$.

Number of accidents in the last 3 years

	0	1	2+	Totals
Under 21 yrs	39 45.57	19 18.67	26 19.76	84
21 - under 25	26 24.41	11 10.00	8 10.59	45
25 yrs and over	18 13.02	4 5.33	2 5.65	24
Totals	83	34	36	153

$$\chi^2 = \sum \frac{(O-E)^2}{E}$$

$\approx 0.947 + 0.006 + 1.971$

$+ 0.104 + 0.100 + 0.633$

$+ 1.905 + 0.332 + 2.358$

$= 8.356$

Step 4: $df = (r-1)(c-1) = 2*2 = 4$

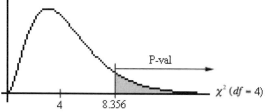

$P - val \approx \chi^2 cdf\left(8.356, 1*10^{99}, 4\right)$

≈ 0.0794

Step 5: $P - val \approx 0.0794 > \alpha \Rightarrow$ Do Not Reject H_o (Too risky)

Step 6: There is not enough evidence, at the 5% significance level, to show that the number of accidents in the last 3 years is dependent on the age of the student.

b) We were actually unable to show dependence in this situation. So anything we notice in the percentages in this problem may well just be due to the chance involved in taking a random sample, rather than indicating any actual trends in age vs. accidents.

37) a) Step 1:
H_o: the responses are independent of the political affiliation of the respondent.
H_a: the responses are dependent on the political affiliation of the respondent.
Step 2: $\alpha = 0.05$
Step 3: Calculate the expected frequencies

for each cell using the formula: $E = \dfrac{R \cdot C}{n}$.

Appropriate to criticize?

	Yes	No	Don't Know	Totals
Repub	149 224.02	257 175.72	8 14.26	414
Democ	275 209.41	93 164.26	19 13.33	387
Indep	63 53.57	32 42.02	4 3.41	99
Totals	487	382	31	900

$$\chi^2 = \sum \frac{(O-E)^2}{E}$$

$\approx 25.123 + 37.596 + 2.748$

$+ 20.544 + 30.914 + 2.412$

$+ 1.660 + 2.389 + 0.012$

$= 123.488$

Step 4: $df = (r-1)(c-1) = 2*2 = 4$

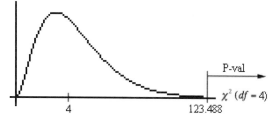

$P - val \approx \chi^2 cdf\left(123.488, 1*10^{99}, 4\right)$

≈ 0.0000

Step 5: $P - val \approx 0.0000 \leq \alpha \Rightarrow$ Reject H_o
(Acceptable risk of making a type I error)
Step 6: There is not enough evidence, at the 5% significance level, to show that the responses are dependent on the political affiliation of the respondent.

b) 71.06% of the democrats thought it was appropriate for the retired generals to criticize the secretary of defense during wartime. This was the largest percentage for any of the parties.

Section 11.1

1) A sample contains paired data if each data value for one variable naturally <u>corresponds</u> to a value for the other variable.

2) $\mu_1 - \mu_2 < 0 \Rightarrow \mu_1$ is <u>smaller</u> than μ_2.
    $\mu_1 - \mu_2 > 0 \Rightarrow \mu_1$ is <u>larger</u> than μ_2.

3) a) $t = \dfrac{\bar{d}}{s_d / \sqrt{n}} = \dfrac{14.25}{31.185 / \sqrt{12}} \approx 1.583$

    b) $H_a : \mu_1 > \mu_2 \Rightarrow$ This is a right-tailed test. $df = n - 1 = 11$

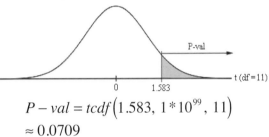

    $P - val = tcdf\left(1.583,\ 1*10^{99},\ 11\right)$
    ≈ 0.0709

    c) $P - val \approx 0.0709 > \alpha \Rightarrow$ Do Not Reject H_o
    (Too Risky)

5) a) $t = \dfrac{\bar{d}}{s_d / \sqrt{n}} = \dfrac{-22.88}{61.007 / \sqrt{40}} \approx -2.372$

    b) $H_a : \mu_1 \neq \mu_2 \Rightarrow$ This is a two-tailed test.
    $df = n - 1 = 39$

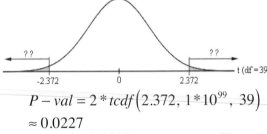

    $P - val = 2 * tcdf\left(2.372,\ 1*10^{99},\ 39\right)$
    ≈ 0.0227

    c) $P - val \approx 0.0227 \leq \alpha \Rightarrow$ Reject H_o
    (Acceptable risk of making a type I error)

7) a) Step 1: We want to show that the average is "lower" after than before the drug.
    $H_o : \mu_1 \leq \mu_2$
    $H_a : \mu_1 > \mu_2$
    Step 2: $\alpha = 0.05$

Step 3: Since $\bar{d}$ is not given, we will find it using the calculator. Enter the before values into L1 and the after values into L2. Then let L3 = L2 – L1. Finally choose STAT > CALC > 1-Var Stats L3 and we get:
$\bar{d} = 47.0$, $s_d \approx 25.640$, $n = 14$
$t = \dfrac{\bar{d}}{s_d / \sqrt{n}} = \dfrac{47.0}{25.64 / \sqrt{14}} \approx 6.859$

Step 4: $H_a : \mu_1 > \mu_2 \Rightarrow$ This is a right-tailed test. $df = n - 1 = 13$

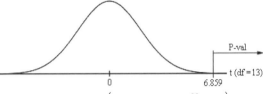

$P - val = tcdf\left(6.859,\ 1*10^{99},\ 13\right)$
≈ 0.0000

Step 5: $P - val \approx 0.0000 \leq \alpha \Rightarrow$ Reject H_o (Acceptable risk of making a type I error)
Step 6: There is enough evidence, at the 5% significance level, to show that the drug will lower, on average, the level of bad cholesterol in patients who take it.

b) We need the t-scores for 90% confidence.

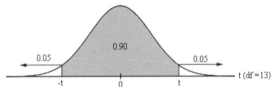

From the t-table with df = 13, we get
$t_{0.05} = 1.771$.
$\bar{d} \pm t \cdot \dfrac{s_d}{\sqrt{n}} = 47.0 \pm 1.771 \cdot \dfrac{25.64}{\sqrt{14}} =$
$47.0 \pm 12.1 \Rightarrow \mu_1 - \mu_2 \in \left(34.9,\ 59.1\right)$

c) We are 90% confident that the average bad cholesterol level after treatment is somewhere between 34.9 and 59.1 points lower than before the treatment.

d) If $\mu_1 - \mu_2 \in (34.9,\ 59.1) \Rightarrow \mu_1 - \mu_2 > 0$
    $\Rightarrow \mu_1 > \mu_2 \Rightarrow H_o : \mu_1 \leq \mu_2$ is false
    $\Rightarrow$ Reject H_o

e) Since $n = 14 < 15$, we must hope that the before and after differences in the population are normally distributed.

9) a) Step 1: We are trying to show a "difference", so we get:

$$H_o : \mu_1 = \mu_2$$
$$H_a : \mu_1 \neq \mu_2$$

Step 2: $\alpha = 0.10$

Step 3: Since $\overline{d}$ is not given, we will find it using the calculator. Enter the before values into L1 and the after values into L2. Then let L3 = L2 – L1. Finally choose STAT > CALC > 1-Var Stats L3 and we get:

$$\overline{d} \approx 0.91667, \; s_d \approx 2.7455, \; n = 12$$

$$t = \frac{\overline{d}}{s_d / \sqrt{n}} = \frac{0.91667}{2.7455 / \sqrt{12}} \approx 1.157$$

Note: It is a good idea to use more decimals than normal for $\overline{d}$ when calculating the test statistic. This helps avoid rounding error.

Step 4: $H_a : \mu_1 \neq \mu_2 \Rightarrow$ This is a two-tailed test. $df = n - 1 = 11$

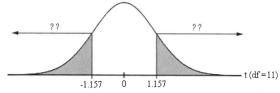

$$P - val = 2 * tcdf\left(1.157, \; 1 * 10^{99}, \; 11\right)$$
$$\approx 0.2718$$

Step 5: $P - val \approx 0.2718 > \alpha \Rightarrow$ Do Not Reject H_o (Too Risky)

Step 6: There is not enough evidence, at the 10% significance level, to show that there is a difference in average score at the two courses for pro players.

b) We need the t-scores for 90% confidence.

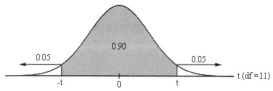

From the t-table with df = 11, we get $t_{0.05} = 1.796$.

$$\overline{d} \pm t \cdot \frac{s_d}{\sqrt{n}} = 0.92 \pm 1.796 \cdot \frac{2.7455}{\sqrt{12}} =$$

$$0.92 \pm 1.42 \Rightarrow \mu_1 - \mu_2 \in \left(-0.50, \; 2.34\right)$$

Note: It is typically fine to use less decimal places for $\overline{d}$ when computing a confidence interval.

c) We are 90% confident that the average score at Poppy Hills is somewhere between 0.50 strokes lower than the average at Spyglass to 2.34 strokes higher than the average at Spyglass.

d) If $\mu_1 - \mu_2 \in \left(-0.50, 2.34\right) \Rightarrow \mu_1 - \mu_2$ could be equal zero $\Rightarrow \mu_1$ could equal $\Rightarrow H_o : \mu_1 = \mu_2$ could be true $\Rightarrow$ Do Not Reject H_o.

e) Since $n = 12 < 30$, we must hope that the differences between Poppy Hills and Spyglass Hill in the population are normally distributed.

f) Because we did not reject H_o, it is possible that we have made a type II error. This is the case if H_o turns out to be a false claim.

11) Givens: $n = 31$, $\overline{d} \approx -0.226$, $s_d \approx 1.820$

a) Step 1: The want to see if the sales after are "higher" than before, so we get

$$H_o : \mu_1 \geq \mu_2$$
$$H_a : \mu_1 < \mu_2$$

Step 2: $\alpha = 0.05$

Step 3: $t = \frac{\overline{d}}{s_d / \sqrt{n}} = \frac{-0.226}{1.82 / \sqrt{31}} \approx -0.691$

Step 4: $H_a : \mu_1 < \mu_2 \Rightarrow$ This is a left-tailed test. $df = n - 1 = 30$

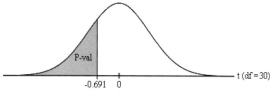

$$P - val = tcdf\left(-1 * 10^{99}, \; -0.691, \; 30\right)$$
$$\approx 0.2474$$

Step 5: $P - val \approx 0.2474 > \alpha \Rightarrow$ Do Not Reject H_o (Too risky)

Step 6: There is not enough evidence, at the 5% significance level, to show that there is, on average, a larger number of units sold by all the sales personnel after the incentive plan.

b) We need the t-score for 90% confidence.

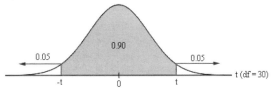

From the t-table with df = 30, we get
$t_{0.05} = 1.697$.

$$\bar{d} \pm t \cdot \frac{s_d}{\sqrt{n}} = -0.226 \pm 1.697 \cdot \frac{1.82}{\sqrt{31}} =$$
$$-0.226 \pm 0.555 \Rightarrow \mu_1 - \mu_2 \in \left(-0.781, \; 0.329\right)$$

c) We are 90% confident that the average number of units sold by the sales personnel with the incentive plan is somewhere between 7.81 units higher and 0.329 units lower than the average before the plan.

d) If $\mu_1 - \mu_2 \in \left(-0.781, 0.329\right) \Rightarrow \mu_1 - \mu_2$ could be equal to zero $\Rightarrow \mu_1$ could equal μ_2 $\Rightarrow H_o : \mu_1 \geq \mu_2$ could be true $\Rightarrow$ Do Not Reject H_o.

e) Since $n = 31 \geq 30$, we know that $\bar{d}$ is normally distributed. So the requirements have been met.

f) $\mu_1 - \mu_2 = 0.53 \Rightarrow \mu_1 > \mu_2 \Rightarrow H_o : \mu_1 \geq \mu_2$ is true. In part (a), we decided not to reject H_o. Therefore, we have made a correct decision.

13) Givens: $n = 25$, $\bar{d} \approx -18.12$, $s_d \approx 11.322$

a) Step 1: We want to show that the average is "better" after the passing the practice
quiz than it was before.
$$H_o : \mu_1 \geq \mu_2$$
$$H_a : \mu_1 < \mu_2$$

Step 2: $\alpha = 0.01$

Step 3: $t = \dfrac{\bar{d}}{s_d \big/ \sqrt{n}} = \dfrac{-18.12}{11.322 \big/ \sqrt{25}} \approx -8.002$

Step 4: $H_a : \mu_1 < \mu_2 \Rightarrow$ This is a left-tailed test. $df = n - 1 = 24$

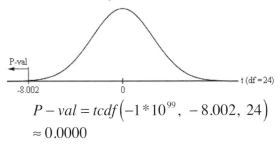

$$P - val = tcdf\left(-1 * 10^{99}, \; -8.002, \; 24\right)$$
$$\approx 0.0000$$

Step 5: $P - val \approx 0.0000 \leq \alpha \Rightarrow$ Reject H_o (Acceptable risk of making a type I error)
Step 6: There is enough evidence, at the 1% significance level, to show that the students, on average, do better after having passed the practice quiz.

b) We need the t-scores for 98% confidence.

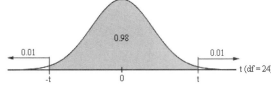

From the t-table with df = 24, we get
$t_{0.01} = 2.492$.

$$\bar{d} \pm t \cdot \frac{s_d}{\sqrt{n}} = -18.12 \pm 2.492 \cdot \frac{11.322}{\sqrt{25}} =$$
$$-18.12 \pm 5.64 \Rightarrow \mu_1 - \mu_2 \in \left(-23.76, \; -12.48\right)$$

c) We are 98% confident that the average quiz score after passing the practice quiz is somewhere between 12.48 and 23.76 points higher than before the practice quiz.

d) If $\mu_1 - \mu_2 \in \left(-23.76, -12.48\right)$ $\Rightarrow \mu_1 - \mu_2 < 0 \Rightarrow \mu_1 < \mu_2$ $\Rightarrow H_o : \mu_1 \geq \mu_2$ is false $\Rightarrow$ Reject H_o

e) Since $15 \leq n = 25 < 30$, we must hope that the before and after differences in the population are not severely skewed.

f) A type I error would occur if we had enough evidence to show that the average scores were lower after the practice quiz, when in fact, they actually were not.

g) A type II error would occur if we did not have enough evidence to show that the average scores were lower after the practice quiz, when in fact, they actually were lower.

Section 11.2

15) Independent samples from two populations have no natural <u>correspondence</u> from one sample to the other. They might not even have the same sample <u>size</u>.

16) Because the df formula in this section is so complicated, it is good to have an <u>estimate</u> of the size of your answer. Use the fact that $\min\{n_1, n_2\} - 1 \le df \le n_1 + n_2 - 2$ to help with this.

17) a) $t = \dfrac{15.392 - 13.899}{\sqrt{\dfrac{3.908^2}{19} + \dfrac{2.471^2}{14}}} \approx 1.341$

On the calculator, this is entered as:

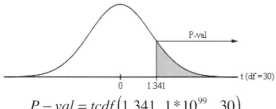

(15.392-13.899)/
√(3.908²/19+2.47
1²/14)
             1.340783102

b) $H_a : \mu_1 > \mu_2 \Rightarrow$ This is a right-tailed test.

$$df = \frac{\left(\dfrac{3.908^2}{19} + \dfrac{2.471^2}{14}\right)^2}{\dfrac{\left(\dfrac{3.908^2}{19}\right)^2}{18} + \dfrac{\left(\dfrac{2.471^2}{14}\right)^2}{13}} \approx 30.43$$

(3.908²/19+2.471
²/14)²/((3.908²/
19)²/18+(2.471²/
14)²/13)
             30.42859392

We round this down and get $df = 30$.

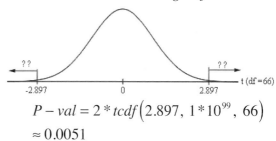

$P - val = tcdf\left(1.341, \, 1 * 10^{99}, \, 30\right)$

≈ 0.0950

c) $P - val \approx 0.0950 > \alpha \Rightarrow$ Do Not Reject H_o
   (Too risky)

19) a) $t = \dfrac{1.537 - 1.209}{\sqrt{\dfrac{0.5081^2}{35} + \dfrac{0.4366^2}{35}}} \approx 2.897$

On the calculator, this is entered as:

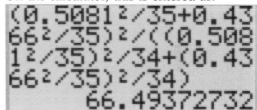

(1.537-1.209)/√(
0.5081²/35+0.436
6²/35)
             2.896600606

b) $H_a : \mu_1 \neq \mu_2 \Rightarrow$ This is a two-tailed test.

$$df = \frac{\left(\dfrac{0.5081^2}{35} + \dfrac{0.4366^2}{35}\right)^2}{\dfrac{\left(\dfrac{0.5081^2}{35}\right)^2}{34} + \dfrac{\left(\dfrac{0.4366^2}{35}\right)^2}{34}} \approx 66.49$$

On the calculator, this is entered as:

(0.5081²/35+0.43
66²/35)²/((0.508
1²/35)²/34+(0.43
66²/35)²/34)
             66.49372732

We round this down and get $df = 66$.

$P - val = 2 * tcdf\left(2.897, \, 1 * 10^{99}, \, 66\right)$

≈ 0.0051

c) $P - val \approx 0.0051 \le \alpha \Rightarrow$ Reject H_o
   (Acceptable risk of making a type I error)

21) Givens: Sample 1 (Bay Area), $n_1 = 27$, $\bar{x}_1 = 3.541$, $s_1 = 0.176$. Sample 2 (Statewide), $n_2 = 60$, $\bar{x}_2 = 3.387$, $s_2 = 0.1625$.

a) Step 1: We want to show that the bay area average is "larger", so we get:
$$H_o : \mu_1 \leq \mu_2$$
$$H_a : \mu_1 > \mu_2$$

Step 2: $\alpha = 0.05$

Step 3:
$$t = \frac{3.541 - 3.387}{\sqrt{0.176^2 / 27 + 0.1625^2 / 60}} \approx 3.865$$

On the calculator, this is entered as:

```
(3.541-3.387)/√(
0.176²/27+0.1625
²/60)
          3.865294031
```

Step 4: $H_a : \mu_1 > \mu_2 \Rightarrow$ This is a right-tailed test.

$$df = \frac{\left(0.176^2 / 27 + 0.1625^2 / 60\right)^2}{\dfrac{\left(0.176^2 / 27\right)^2}{26} + \dfrac{\left(0.1625^2 / 60\right)^2}{59}} \approx 46.74$$

On the calculator, this is entered as:

```
(0.176²/27+0.162
5²/60)²/((0.176²
/27)²/26+(0.1625
²/60)²/59)
          46.74278227
```

We round this down and get $df = 46$.

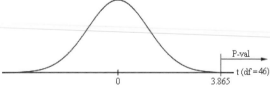

$$P-val = tcdf\left(3.865, 1*10^{99}, 46\right)$$
$$\approx 0.0002$$

Step 5: $P-val \approx 0.0002 \leq \alpha \Rightarrow$ Reject H_o (Acceptable risk of making a type I error)

Step 6: There is enough evidence, at the 5% significance level, to show that the average gas price in the bay area is higher than the statewide average.

b) We need the t-scores for 90% confidence. We will also round our df down to 45 because 46 is not on the t-table.

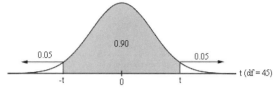

From the t-table we get $t_{0.05} = 1.679$.

$$\left(3.541 - 3.387\right) \pm 1.679 \cdot \sqrt{\frac{0.176^2}{27} + \frac{0.1625^2}{60}} =$$
$$0.154 \pm 0.067 \Rightarrow \mu_1 - \mu_2 \in \left(0.087, 0.221\right)$$

Note: The margin of error is entered in the calculator as:

```
1.679*√(0.176²/2
7+0.1625²/60)
          .0668942642
```

c) We are 90% confident that the average price per gallon in the bay area is somewhere between 8.7 and 22.1 cents more expensive than the statewide average.

d) If $\mu_1 - \mu_2 \in (0.087, 0.221) \Rightarrow \mu_1 - \mu_2 > 0$
$\Rightarrow \mu_1 > \mu_2 \Rightarrow H_o : \mu_1 \leq \mu_2$ is false
$\Rightarrow$ Reject H_o

e) Bay Area: $15 \leq n_1 = 27 < 30 \Rightarrow$ We need a population for gas prices in the bay area that is not severely skewed.
Statewide: $n_2 = 60 \geq 30 \Rightarrow \bar{x}_1$ is normally distributed regardless of the distribution of the population.

f) Since we Rejected H_o, we know we did not make a type II error. If H_o is true, then we have made a type I error. If H_o is false, then we have made a correct decision.

23) a) Step 1: We are trying to show that there is a difference in the means.

$$H_o : \mu_1 = \mu_2$$
$$H_a : \mu_1 \neq \mu_2$$

Step 2: $\alpha = 0.05$

Step 3:

$$t = \frac{1394.6 - 1524.3}{\sqrt{\dfrac{282.75^2}{126} + \dfrac{226.65^2}{81}}} \approx -3.641$$

Step 4: $H_a : \mu_1 \neq \mu_2 \Rightarrow$ This is a two-tailed test.

$$df = \frac{\left(\dfrac{282.75^2}{126} + \dfrac{226.65^2}{81}\right)^2}{\dfrac{\left(\dfrac{282.75^2}{126}\right)^2}{125} + \dfrac{\left(\dfrac{226.65^2}{81}\right)^2}{80}} \approx 195.14$$

??   ??
-3.641   0   3.641   t (df =195)

$$P - val = 2 * tcdf\left(3.641,\ 1 * 10^{99},\ 195\right)$$
$$\approx 0.0003$$

Step 5: $P - val \approx 0.0003 \leq \alpha \Rightarrow$ Reject H_o (Acceptable risk of making a type I error)

Step 6: There is enough evidence, at the 5% significance level, to show that there is a difference between the average combined SAT scores of public and private schools students.

b) We need the t-scores for 95% confidence. We will round our df down to 100, because 195 is not on the t-table.

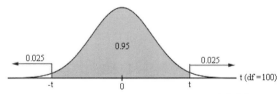

0.025   0.95   0.025
-t   0   t   t (df = 100)

From the t-table we get $t_{0.025} = 1.984$.

$$\left(1394.6 - 1524.3\right) \pm 1.984 \cdot \sqrt{\frac{282.75^2}{126} + \frac{226.65^2}{81}} =$$
$$-129.7 \pm 70.7 \Rightarrow \mu_1 - \mu_2 \in (-200.4,\ -59.0)$$

c) We are 95% confident that average combined SAT score for private schools students is somewhere between 59.0 points and 200.4 points above that of the public school students.

d) If
$$\mu_1 - \mu_2 \in (-200.4,\ -59.0) \Rightarrow \mu_1 - \mu_2 < 0$$
$$\Rightarrow \mu_1 < \mu_2 \Rightarrow H_o : \mu_1 = \mu_2 \text{ is false}$$
$$\Rightarrow \text{Reject } H_o$$

e) $\mu_1 - \mu_2 = -9.9 \Rightarrow \mu_1 \neq \mu_2 \Rightarrow H_o : \mu_1 = \mu_2$ is false. In part (a), we decided to reject H_o. Therefore, we have made a correct decision.

25) a) Step 1: We are trying to show that there is a "difference", so we get:

$$H_o : \mu_1 = \mu_2$$
$$H_a : \mu_1 \neq \mu_2$$

Step 2: $\alpha = 0.01$

Step 3: Since we have only been given the sample data, we must use it to find the means and standard deviations that we need. Do this one sample at a time. Enter the California prices into L1. Then choose STAT > CALC > 1-Var Stats L1. This yields:

$n_1 = 16,\ \overline{x}_1 = 55.6875,\ s_1 \approx 15.226$

Repeating this process with the Colorado prices produces the following results:

$n_2 = 12,\ \overline{x}_2 = 65.8333,\ s_2 \approx 16.275$

$$t = \frac{55.6875 - 65.8333}{\sqrt{\dfrac{15.226^2}{16} + \dfrac{16.275^2}{12}}} \approx -1.678$$

Step 4: $H_a : \mu_1 \neq \mu_2 \Rightarrow$ This is a two-tailed test.

$$df = \frac{\left(\dfrac{15.226^2}{16} + \dfrac{16.275^2}{12}\right)^2}{\dfrac{\left(\dfrac{15.226^2}{16}\right)^2}{15} + \dfrac{\left(\dfrac{16.275^2}{12}\right)^2}{11}} \approx 22.93$$

??   ??
-1.678   0   1.678   t (df =22)

$$P - val = 2 * tcdf\left(1.678,\ 1 * 10^{99},\ 22\right)$$
$$\approx 0.1075$$

Step 5: $P - val \approx 0.1075 > \alpha \Rightarrow$ Do Not Reject H_o (Too risky)

Step 6: There is not enough evidence, at the 1% significance level, to show that there is a difference in average adult lift ticket price between California and Colorado resorts.

b) California: $15 \leq n_1 = 16 < 30 \Rightarrow$ We need a population for adult lift ticket prices that is not severely skewed.
Colorado: $n_2 = 12 < 30 \Rightarrow$ We need the prices of adult lift tickets in Colorado to be normally distributed.

c) We need to find the t-scores for 99% confidence with df = 22.

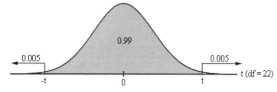

From the t-table we get $t_{0.005} = 2.819$.

$$\left(55.6875 - 65.8333\right) \pm 2.819 \cdot \sqrt{\frac{15.226^2}{16} + \frac{16.275^2}{12}} =$$

$$-10.14 \pm 17.05 \Rightarrow \mu_1 - \mu_2 \in \left(-27.19, \, 6.91\right)$$

d) We are 99% confident that, on average, adult lift tickets at California resorts are somewhere between $27.19 less and $6.91 higher than those in Colorado.

e) If $\mu_1 - \mu_2 \in \left(-27.19, \, 6.91\right) \Rightarrow \mu_1 - \mu_2$ could be equal to zero $\Rightarrow \mu_1$ could equal $\mu_2 \Rightarrow H_o : \mu_1 = \mu_2$ could be true $\Rightarrow$ Do Not Reject H_o.

Section 11.3

27) The requirements for two-sample proportion studies are that each <u>sample</u> must contain a t least 5 <u>successes</u> and at least 5 <u>failures</u>.

28) $p_1 - p_2 < 0 \Rightarrow p_1$ is <u>smaller</u> than p_2.
$p_1 - p_2 > 0 \Rightarrow p_1$ is <u>larger</u> than p_2.

29) a) $\hat{p}_1 = \frac{122}{195} \approx 0.6256$, $\quad \hat{p}_2 = \frac{89}{147} \approx 0.6054$,

$$\hat{p}_p = \frac{122 + 89}{195 + 147} \approx 0.6170$$

$$z = \frac{0.6256 - 0.6054}{\sqrt{0.617 * 0.383\left(\frac{1}{195} + \frac{1}{147}\right)}} \approx 0.380$$

On the calculator, this is entered as:

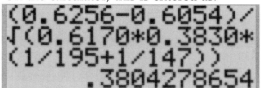

b) $H_a : p_1 > p_2 \Rightarrow$ This is a right-tailed test.

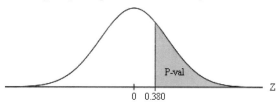

$$P - val = normalcdf\left(0.380, \, 1 * 10^{99}\right)$$
$$\approx 0.3520$$

c) $P - val \approx 0.3520 > \alpha \Rightarrow$ Do Not Reject H_o (Too risky)

31) a) $\hat{p}_1 = \frac{350}{675} \approx 0.5185$, $\quad \hat{p}_2 = \frac{309}{692} \approx 0.4465$,

$$\hat{p}_p = \frac{350 + 309}{675 + 692} \approx 0.4821$$

$$z = \frac{0.5185 - 0.4465}{\sqrt{0.4821 * 0.5179\left(\frac{1}{675} + \frac{1}{692}\right)}} \approx 2.664$$

On the calculator, this is entered as:

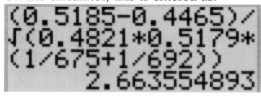

b) $H_a : p_1 \neq p_2 \Rightarrow$ This is a two-tailed test.

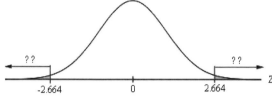

$$P - val = 2 * normalcdf\left(2.664, \ 1*10^{99}\right)$$

$$\approx 0.0077$$

c) $P - val \approx 0.0077 \leq \alpha \Rightarrow$ Reject H_o
(Acceptable risk of making a type I error)

33) Givens:

Sample 1 (America): $x_1 = 157$, $n_1 = 419$

Sample 2 (Canada): $x_2 = 151$, $n_2 = 387$

a) Step 1: We are trying to show a

"difference", so we get: $\quad H_o : p_1 = p_2$
$\quad\quad\quad\quad\quad\quad\quad\quad\quad H_a : p_1 \neq p_2$

Step 2: $\alpha = 0.05$

Step 3: $\hat{p}_1 = \dfrac{157}{419} \approx 0.3747$,

$\hat{p}_2 = \dfrac{151}{387} \approx 0.3902$,

$\hat{p}_p = \dfrac{157+151}{419+387} \approx 0.3821$

$$z = \dfrac{0.3747 - 0.3902}{\sqrt{0.3821 * 0.6179\left(\dfrac{1}{419} + \dfrac{1}{387}\right)}} \approx -0.452$$

On the calculator, this is entered as:

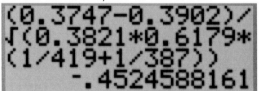

Step 4: $H_a : p_1 \neq p_2 \Rightarrow$ This is a two-tailed test.

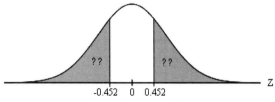

$$P - val = 2 * normalcdf\left(0.452, \ 1*10^{99}\right)$$

$$\approx 0.6513$$

Step 5: $P - val \approx 0.6513 > \alpha \Rightarrow$ Do Not Reject H_o (Too risky)

Step 6: There is not enough evidence, at the 5% significance level, to show that there is a difference in the proportion of people with type O+ blood between the U.S. and Canada.

b) We need the z-scores for 95% confidence.

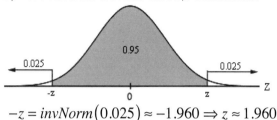

$$-z = invNorm(0.025) \approx -1.960 \Rightarrow z \approx 1.960$$

$$(0.3747 - 0.3902) \pm 1.96 \cdot \sqrt{\dfrac{0.3747 * 0.6253}{419} + \dfrac{0.3902 * 0.6098}{387}} =$$

$$-0.0155 \pm 0.0672 \Rightarrow p_1 - p_2 \in (-0.0827, \ 0.0517)$$

Note: On the calculator, the margin of error piece is entered as shown below.

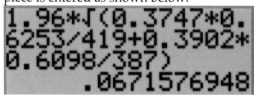

c) We are 95% confident that the proportion of people in the U.S with type O+ blood is somewhere between 8.27% less and 5.17% more than the proportion in Canada.

d) If $p_1 - p_2 \in (-0.0827, \ 0.0517) \Rightarrow p_1 - p_2$ could be equal to zero $\Rightarrow p_1$ could equal $p_2 \Rightarrow H_o : p_1 = p_2$ could be true $\Rightarrow$ Do Not Reject H_o.

e) There were at least 5 people with type O+ blood and without type O+ blood in each sample, so the requirements have been met.

f) Since we did not reject $H_o \Rightarrow$ that it is possible that we have made a type II error. This has occurred only if H_o is actually false.

35) Givens:

Sample 1 (HF Laws): $x_1 = 259$, $n_1 = 473$

Sample 2 (No HF Laws): $x_2 = 235$, $n_2 = 831$

a) Step 1: We are trying to show that the proportion is "higher" in the states with the hands free laws, so we get:

$$H_o : p_1 \le p_2$$
$$H_a : p_1 > p_2$$

Step 2: $\alpha = 0.01$

Step 3: $\hat{p}_1 = \dfrac{259}{473} \approx 0.5476$,

$\hat{p}_2 = \dfrac{235}{831} \approx 0.2828$,

$\hat{p}_p = \dfrac{259 + 235}{473 + 831} \approx 0.3788$

$$z = \dfrac{0.5476 - 0.2828}{\sqrt{0.3788 * 0.6212 \left(\dfrac{1}{473} + \dfrac{1}{831} \right)}} \approx 9.477$$

Step 4: $H_a : p_1 > p_2 \Rightarrow$ This is a right-tailed test.

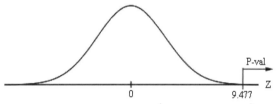

$$P - val = normalcdf\left(9.477, 1*10^{99}\right)$$
$$\approx 0.0000$$

Step 5: $P - val \approx 0.0000 \le \alpha \Rightarrow$ Reject H_o (Acceptable risk of making a type I error)

Step 6: There is enough evidence, at the 1% significance level, to show that the proportion of use of hands-free devices while driving is higher in states that have laws requiring them.

b) We need the z-scores for 98% confidence.

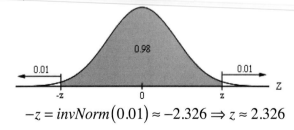

$$-z = invNorm(0.01) \approx -2.326 \Rightarrow z \approx 2.326$$

$$(0.5476 - 0.2828) \pm 2.326 \cdot \sqrt{\dfrac{0.5476 * 0.4524}{473} + \dfrac{0.2828 * 0.7172}{831}} =$$

$$0.2648 \pm 0.0645 \Rightarrow p_1 - p_2 \in (0.2003, 0.3293)$$

c) We are 98% confident that the proportion of people that use a hands-free device in states that require them is somewhere between 20.03% and 32.93% higher than in states that do not.

d) If $p_1 - p_2 \in (0.2003, 0.3293)$
$\Rightarrow p_1 - p_2 > 0 \Rightarrow p_1 > p_2 \Rightarrow H_o : p_1 \le p_2$
is false $\Rightarrow$ Reject H_o.

e) There were at least 5 people using and not using hands-free devices in each sample, so the requirements have been met.

f) A type I error would occur if we had enough evidence to show that a higher proportion of the people in states with hands-free than people in states with such laws use such a device, when in fact the proportion is not higher.

37) Givens:

Sample 1 (Men): $\hat{p}_1 \approx 0.132$, $n_1 = 258$

Sample 2: (Women): $\hat{p}_2 \approx 0.104$, $n_2 = 241$

a) Step 1: We are trying to show a "difference", so we get:

$$H_o : p_1 = p_2$$
$$H_a : p_1 \ne p_2$$

Step 2: $\alpha = 0.10$

Step 3: This time, we were given the sample proportions rather than the number of successes in each sample. This seems like a head start, but we actually need the number of successes in each sample to calculate the value of $\hat{p}_p$.

$x_1 = n_1 \cdot \hat{p}_1 = 258(0.132) = 34.056 \Rightarrow$
$x_1 = 34$

$x_2 = n_2 \cdot \hat{p}_2 = 241(0.104) = 25.064 \Rightarrow$
$x_2 = 25$

$\hat{p}_p = \dfrac{34 + 25}{258 + 241} \approx 0.1182$

$$z = \dfrac{0.132 - 0.104}{\sqrt{0.1182 * 0.8818 \left(\dfrac{1}{258} + \dfrac{1}{241} \right)}} \approx 0.968$$

Step 4: $H_a : p_1 \neq p_2 \Rightarrow$ This is a two-tailed test.

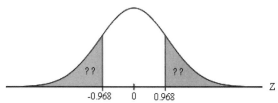

$$P - val = 2 * normalcdf(0.968, 1*10^{99})$$

$$\approx 0.3330$$

Step 5: $P - val \approx 0.3330 > \alpha \Rightarrow$ Do Not Reject H_o (Too risky)

Step 6: There is not enough evidence, at the 10% significance level, to show that there is a difference in the proportion of men and women that live in cell phone only households.

b) There were at least 5 people with type O+ blood and without type O+ blood in each sample, so the requirements have been met.

c) We need the z-scores for 90% confidence.

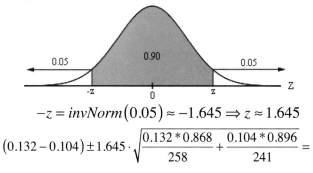

$$-z = invNorm(0.05) \approx -1.645 \Rightarrow z \approx 1.645$$

$$(0.132 - 0.104) \pm 1.645 \cdot \sqrt{\frac{0.132*0.868}{258} + \frac{0.104*0.896}{241}} =$$

$$0.2648 \pm 0.0645 \Rightarrow p_1 - p_2 \in (-0.019, 0.075)$$

d) We are 90% confident that the proportion of men living in cell phone only households is somewhere between 1.9% less and 7.5% more than the proportion of women in such households.

e) If $p_1 - p_2 \in (-0.019, 0.075) \Rightarrow p_1 - p_2$ could be equal to zero $\Rightarrow p_1$ could equal $p_2 \Rightarrow H_o : p_1 = p_2$ could be true $\Rightarrow$ Do Not Reject H_o.

<u>Cumulative Review: Chapters 8 – 11</u>

1) a) We start by using the data to find the mean and standard deviation. Since this is sample data, we will use $\bar{x}$ and s. Using the calculator, enter the data into L1. Then, choose STAT > CALC > 1-Var Stats L1 and press enter. This gives us:
$\bar{x} \approx 15.13$, $s \approx 2.3220$, $n = 18$
We need the t-scores for 90% confidence with $df = n - 1 = 17$.

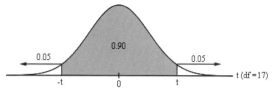

From the t-table we find $t_{0.05} = 1.740$.

$$\bar{x} \pm t \cdot \frac{s}{\sqrt{n}} = 15.13 \pm 1.74 \cdot \frac{2.322}{\sqrt{18}} =$$
$$15.13 \pm 0.95 \Rightarrow \mu \in (14.18,\ 16.08)$$

b) The margin of error is the part that we add and subtract to get the interval. So, E = 0.95 years.

c) We are 90% confident that the mean lifespan of all house cats is somewhere between 14.18 and 16.08 years.

d) Since $15 \le n = 18 < 30$, we must hope that the population of life spans is not severely skewed.

e) When calculating sample size, we always use z-scores. Therefore, we must find the z-scores for 90% confidence.

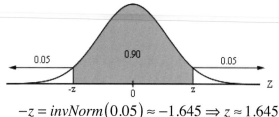

$$-z = invNorm(0.05) \approx -1.645 \Rightarrow z \approx 1.645$$

They are requesting a margin of error of at most 0.25 years, so E = 0.25. σ is unknown, so we will use s in its place.

$$n = \left(\frac{z \cdot \sigma}{E}\right)^2 = \left(\frac{1.645 * 2.322}{0.25}\right)$$
$$\approx 233.44 \Rightarrow n = 234$$

Notes: We always round up when calculating sample size. It may seem strange to use a z-score when σ is unknown, but to use a t-score you need a df. We are trying to find sample size, so we don't know which df to use. These types of questions often result in large sample sizes. For large sample sizes, t-scores and z-scores are almost the same. So, it makes sense to use the z-score in the calculation.

2) Givens: $n = 35$, $\bar{x} = 14.38$, and $\sigma = 2.3$.
   a) Since we know the value of σ, we need to find the z-scores for 95% confidence.

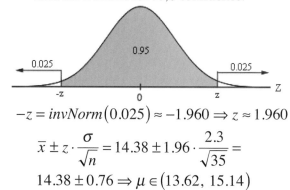

$$-z = invNorm(0.025) \approx -1.960 \Rightarrow z \approx 1.960$$

$$\bar{x} \pm z \cdot \frac{\sigma}{\sqrt{n}} = 14.38 \pm 1.96 \cdot \frac{2.3}{\sqrt{35}} =$$
$$14.38 \pm 0.76 \Rightarrow \mu \in (13.62,\ 15.14)$$

   b) The margin of error is the part we add and subtract, so E = 0.76 years

   c) No, $\mu \in (13.62,\ 15.14) \Rightarrow \mu$ could be 15.1, which is actually more than 15 years.

   d) Since $n = 35 \ge 30$, we know that $\bar{x}$ is normal and the requirements have been met.

   e) They are asking for a margin of error of at most 0.25 years, so E = 0.25.

$$n = \left(\frac{z \cdot \sigma}{E}\right)^2 = \left(\frac{1.960 * 2.3}{0.25}\right) \approx 325.15$$
$$\Rightarrow n = 326$$

3) Givens: $n = 32$, $\bar{x} = 845.82$, and $s = 715.10$.

a) Step 1: The key word "exceeds" indicates that we should use:
$$H_o : \mu \leq 800$$
$$H_a : \mu > 800$$
Step 2: $\alpha = 0.10$

Step 3: Since, σ is unknown, we use a t-score as our test statistic.
$$t = \frac{845.82 - 800}{715.10 / \sqrt{32}} \approx 0.362$$

Step 4: $H_a : \mu > 800 \Rightarrow$ This is a right-tailed test. Also, $df = n - 1 = 31$.

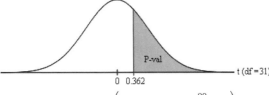

$$P - val = tcdf\left(0.362, 1*10^{99}, 31\right)$$
$$\approx 0.3599$$

Step 5: $P - val \approx 0.3599 \geq \alpha \Rightarrow$ Do Not Reject H_o (Too risky)

Step 6: The data does not provide enough evidence ,at the 10% significance level, to show that the poker player will average more than $800/week in winnings.

b) Since $n = 32 \geq 30$, we know that $\bar{x}$ is normal and the requirements have been met.

c) $\mu = 795 \Rightarrow H_0 : \mu \leq 800$ is true $\Rightarrow$ Not rejecting H_0 was a correct decision.

d) We're not really sure. Since his sample mean was more than $800, that provides evidence that he can. However, we didn't have enough evidence to prove that he could. He is a gambler, so he'll probably take the chance and buy it.

4) Givens: $n = 913$, $x = 568$
$$\Rightarrow \hat{p} = \frac{x}{n} = \frac{568}{913} \approx 0.6221$$

a) Proportion intervals always use z-scores. We need the z-scores for 99% confidence.

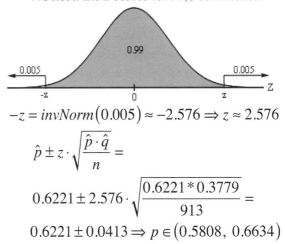

$$-z = invNorm(0.005) \approx -2.576 \Rightarrow z \approx 2.576$$

$$\hat{p} \pm z \cdot \sqrt{\frac{\hat{p} \cdot \hat{q}}{n}} =$$

$$0.6221 \pm 2.576 \cdot \sqrt{\frac{0.6221 * 0.3779}{913}} =$$

$$0.6221 \pm 0.0413 \Rightarrow p \in (0.5808,\ 0.6634)$$

b) The margin of error is the part we are adding and subtracting to get the interval, so E = 0.0413 or 4.13%

c) Yes, $p \in (0.5808,\ 0.6634) \Rightarrow p > 0.50$

d) $x = 568 \geq 5$ and $n - x = 345 \geq 5$. The sample contained at least 5 successes and at least 5 failures, so the requirements have been met.

e) Since we are asked to make a conservative guess at the population proportion, we should use the value from the interval above that is closest to 0.5. So we will use $p_g = 0.5808$. We are asked to have a margin of error of at most 2%, so E = 0.02.

$$n = p_g\left(1 - p_g\right)\left(\frac{z}{E}\right)^2 =$$

$$0.5808 * 0.4192 * \left(\frac{2.576}{0.02}\right)^2 \approx 4039.05$$

$$\Rightarrow n = 4040$$

5) Givens: We are only given sample data, so we must calculate the value of the mean from this. We get: $n = 14$, $\bar{x} \approx 8.7357$.

a) Step 1: We want to show that the mean "exceeds" 8 minutes, so we get: $H_o : \mu \le 8$
$H_a : \mu > 8$

Step 2: $\alpha = 0.05$

Step 3: We are given $\sigma = 3.0952$, so we will use a z-score for our test statistic.

$$z = \frac{8.7357 - 8}{3.0952 / \sqrt{14}} \approx 0.889$$

Step 4: $H_a : \mu > 8 \Rightarrow$ This is a right-tailed test.

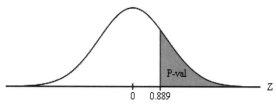

$$P - val = normalcdf\left(0.889, 1*10^{99}\right)$$
$$\approx 0.1870$$

Step 5: $P - val \approx 0.1870 > \alpha \Rightarrow$ Do not reject H_o (too risky)

Step 6: The data did not provide enough evidence, at the 5% significance level, to show that the true average wait time exceeds 8 minutes.

b) Since $n = 14 < 15$, we must hope that the wait times in the population are normally distributed.

c) Since we did not reject H_o, it is possible that we have made a type II error. This is the case if H_o turns out to be a false claim.

d) We need the z-scores for 90% confidence.

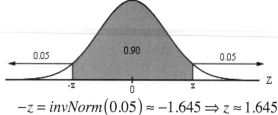

$-z = invNorm(0.05) \approx -1.645 \Rightarrow z \approx 1.645$

$$\bar{x} \pm z \cdot \frac{\sigma}{\sqrt{n}} = 8.7357 \pm 1.645 \cdot \frac{3.0952}{\sqrt{14}} =$$

$8.7357 \pm 1.3608 \Rightarrow \mu \in (7.3749, 10.0965)$

e) $\mu \in (7.3749, 10.0965) \Rightarrow \mu$ could equal 8 $\Rightarrow H_o : \mu \le 8$ could be true Do Not Reject H_o.

6) Givens: $x = 271$, $n = 425$

$$\Rightarrow \hat{p} = \frac{x}{n} = \frac{271}{425} \approx 0.6376$$

a) Step 1: We are trying to show that "more than half" believe this, so $H_o : p \le 0.50$
$H_a : p > 0.50$

Step 2: $\alpha = 0.01$

Step 3: $z = \frac{0.6376 - 0.5}{\sqrt{\frac{0.5 * 0.5}{425}}} \approx 5.673$

Step 4: $H_a : p > 0.5 \Rightarrow$ This is a right-tailed test.

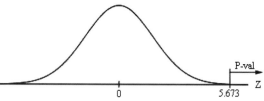

$$P - val = normalcdf\left(5.673, 1*10^{99}\right)$$
$$\approx 0.0000$$

Step 5: $P - val \approx 0.0000 \le \alpha \Rightarrow$ Reject H_o (Acceptable risk of making a type I error)

Step 6: The data does provide enough evidence, at the 1% significance level, to show that the more than half of all Americans believed that Chinese toys were unsafe at that time.

b) We need the z-scores for 98% confidence.

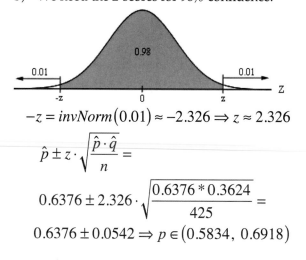

$-z = invNorm(0.01) \approx -2.326 \Rightarrow z \approx 2.326$

$$\hat{p} \pm z \cdot \sqrt{\frac{\hat{p} \cdot \hat{q}}{n}} =$$

$$0.6376 \pm 2.326 \cdot \sqrt{\frac{0.6376 * 0.3624}{425}} =$$

$0.6376 \pm 0.0542 \Rightarrow p \in (0.5834, 0.6918)$

c) $p \in (0.5834, 0.6918) \Rightarrow p > 0.50$ $\Rightarrow H_o : p \le 0.50$ is false $\Rightarrow$ We should reject H_o.

d) $np_0 = 425*0.5 = 212.5 \geq 5$ &

$nq_0 = 425*0.5 = 212.5 \geq 5$, so the requirements have been met for the hypothesis test ; the sample contained at least 5 successes and at least 5 failures, so the requirements have also been met for the confidence interval.

e) A type I error would occur if we had enough evidence to show that more than half of all Americans believe that Chinese toys are unsafe, when in fact the proportion is not more than half.

7) a) Step 1:

H_o : the distribution of education levels in his home town is the same as in the city where he plays football.

H_a : the distribution of education levels in his home town is different than in the city where he plays football.

Step 2: $\alpha = 0.10$

Step 3: The values of O are from the sample, and we convert the given percentages to decimals to get p.

Educ	O	p_i	$E = np_i$	$\dfrac{(O-E)^2}{E}$
No HS	32	0.1658	66.32	17.760
HS	219	0.3454	138.16	47.301
Some C	91	0.2787	111.48	3.762
Bach+	58	0.2101	84.04	8.069
	400	1.000	400	76.892

$$\chi^2 = \sum \frac{(O-E)^2}{E} \approx 76.892$$

Step 4: $df = k - 1 = 3$

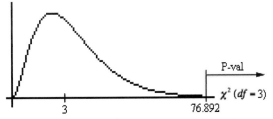

$$P - val = \chi^2 cdf\left(76.982, 1*10^{99}, 3\right) \approx 0.0000$$

Step 5: $P - val \approx 0.0000 \leq \alpha \Rightarrow$ Reject H_o (Acceptable risk of making a type I error)

Step 6: There is enough evidence, at the 10% significance level, to show that the distribution of education levels in his hometown is different than in the city where he plays football.

b) 100% of the E's are at least 5, so the requirements have been met.

c) Since we rejected H_o, it is possible we have made a type I error. This is the case only if H_o is true. We perceive the risk of this to be nearly zero.

d) The high school only category provided the most evidence against H_o, because it contributed the most to the test statistic.

8) a) Step 1:

H_o : the dice are producing these sums in the proper proportions

H_a : the dice are not producing these sums in the proper proportions.

Step 2: $\alpha = 0.01$

Step 3: The values of O are from the sample. The values of p are not given, so we must find them using the normal probabilities for these events. To help find these probabilities, we need to make the chart for all possible sums.

	1	2	3	4	5	6
1	2	3	4	5	6	7
2	3	4	5	6	7	8
3	4	5	6	7	8	9
4	5	6	7	8	9	10
5	6	7	8	9	10	11
6	7	8	9	10	11	12

Sum	O	p_i	$E = np_i$	$\dfrac{(O-E)^2}{E}$
2,3,12	24	4/36	20.56	0.577
7,11	51	8/36	41.11	2.379
Other	110	24/36	123.33	1.441
	185	1.000	185	4.397

$$\chi^2 = \sum \frac{(O-E)^2}{E} \approx 4.397$$

Step 4: $df = k - 1 = 2$

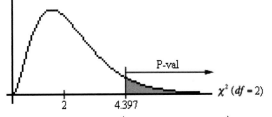

$$P - val = \chi^2 cdf\left(4.397, 1*10^{99}, 2\right) \approx 0.1110$$

Step 5: $P - val \approx 0.1110 > \alpha \Rightarrow$ Do Not Reject H_o (Too risky)

Step 6: There is not enough evidence, at the 1% significance level, to show that the dice are not producing these sums in the proper proportions.

b) All expected frequencies ≥ 5, so the requirements have been met.

c) A type I error would occur if we had enough evidence to show that the dice are not producing these sums in the proper proportions, when in fact they are producing them in the correct proportions.

d) A type II error would occur if we did not have enough evidence to show that the dice are not producing them in the proper proportions, when in fact they are not producing them in the correct proportions.

9) a) Step 1:

H_o: people's opinion on this matter is independent of their political affiliation.
H_a: people's opinion on this matter is dependent on their political affiliation.
Step 2: $\alpha = 0.05$

Step 3: Calculate E's using: $E = \dfrac{R \cdot C}{n}$.

	Dem	Rep	Ind	Totals
Good Idea	62	36	18	116
	51.95	51.14	12.91	
Bad Idea	417	446	103	966
	432.60	425.88	107.52	
Good & Bad	21	10	5	36
	16.12	15.87	4.01	
Not Sure	15	15	2	32
	14.33	14.11	3.56	
Totals	515	507	128	1150

$$\chi^2 = \sum \frac{(O-E)^2}{E}$$

$$\approx 1.944 + 4.482 + 2.007$$
$$+ 0.563 + 0.951 + 0.190$$
$$+ 1.477 + 2.171 + 0.244$$
$$+ 0.031 + 0.056 + 0.684$$
$$= 14.803$$

Step 4: $df = (r-1)(c-1) = 3*2 = 6$

$$P - val = \chi^2 cdf\left(14.803, 1*10^{99}, 6\right) \approx 0.0218$$

Step 5: $P - val \approx 0.0218 \leq \alpha \Rightarrow$ Reject H_o (Acceptable risk of making a type I error)

Step 6: There is enough evidence, at the 5% significance level, to show that people's opinion on this matter is dependent on their political affiliation.

b) $10/12 \approx 83.33\%$ of the expected frequencies are at least 5, and all of the expected frequencies are at least 1, so the requirements have been met.

c) $E = np = n * P(\text{Good Idea \& Democrat})$
$= n * P(\text{Good Idea}) * P(\text{Democrat})$
$\approx 1150 * \dfrac{116}{1150} * \dfrac{515}{1150} \approx 51.95$

10) a) Step 1: We are trying to show that there is a "difference", so we get:
$H_o : \mu_1 = \mu_2$
$H_a : \mu_1 \neq \mu_2$

Step 2: $\alpha = 0.01$

Step 3:

$$t = \frac{134.9 - 141.4}{\sqrt{\dfrac{6.4904^2}{12} + \dfrac{7.2017^2}{9}}} \approx -2.135$$

Step 4: $H_a : \mu_1 \neq \mu_2 \Rightarrow$ This is a two-tailed test.

$$df = \frac{\left(\dfrac{6.4904^2}{12} + \dfrac{7.2017^2}{9}\right)^2}{\dfrac{\left(\dfrac{6.4904^2}{12}\right)^2}{11} + \dfrac{\left(\dfrac{7.2017^2}{9}\right)^2}{8}} \approx 16.31$$

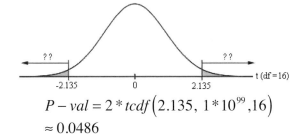

$$P - val = 2 * tcdf\left(2.135, \ 1*10^{99}, 16\right)$$
$$\approx 0.0486$$

Step 5: $P - val \approx 0.0486 > \alpha \Rightarrow$ Do Not Reject H_o (Too risky)

Step 6: There is not enough evidence, at the 1% significance level, to show that there is a difference between the average breaking distance of cars and SUVs.

b) We need the t-scores for 99% confidence.

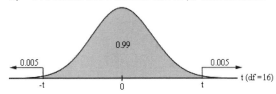

From the t-table, we get $t_{0.005} = 2.921$.

$$\left(134.9 - 141.4\right) \pm 2.921 \cdot \sqrt{\frac{6.4902^2}{12} + \frac{7.2017^2}{9}}$$
$$= -6.5 \pm 8.9 \Rightarrow \mu_1 - \mu_2 \in \left(-15.4, \ 2.4\right)$$

c) We are 99% confident that the average breaking distance for SUVs is somewhere between 2.4 feet less than and 15.4 feet more than the average for cars.

d) If $\mu_1 - \mu_2 \in \left(-15.4, 2.4\right) \Rightarrow \mu_1 - \mu_2$ could be equal to zero $\Rightarrow \mu_1$ could equal $\mu_2 \Rightarrow H_o : \mu_1 = \mu_2$ could be true $\Rightarrow$ Do Not Reject H_o.

e) Cars: $n_2 = 12 < 30 \Rightarrow$ We need the breaking distances for cars to be normally distributed.
SUVs: $n_2 = 9 < 30 \Rightarrow$ We need the breaking distances for SUVs to be normally distributed.

f) $\mu_1 - \mu_2 = -7.7 \Rightarrow \mu_1 \neq \mu_2 \Rightarrow H_o : \mu_1 = \mu_2$ is false $\Rightarrow$ by not rejecting H_o we have made a type II error.

11) Givens:
Sample 1 (18-39): $x_1 = 146$, $n_1 = 212$
Sample 2 (40+): $x_2 = 77$, $n_2 = 219$

a) Step 1: We are trying to show that there is a "difference", so we get:
$$H_o : p_1 = p_2$$
$$H_a : p_1 \neq p_2$$

Step 2: $\alpha = 0.10$

Step 3: $\hat{p}_1 = \dfrac{x_1}{n_1} = \dfrac{146}{212} \approx 0.6887$,

$\hat{p}_2 = \dfrac{x_2}{n_2} = \dfrac{77}{219} \approx 0.3516$,

$\hat{p}_p = \dfrac{x_1 + x_2}{n_1 + n_2} = \dfrac{146 + 77}{212 + 219} \approx 0.5174$

$$z = \frac{0.6887 - 0.3516}{\sqrt{0.5174 * 0.4826\left(\dfrac{1}{212} + \dfrac{1}{219}\right)}} \approx 7.002$$

Step 4: $H_a : p_1 \neq p_2 \Rightarrow$ This is a two-tailed test.

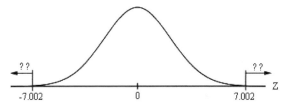

$$P - val = 2 * normalcdf\left(7.002, \ 1*10^{99}\right)$$
$$\approx 0.0000$$

Step 5: $P - val \approx 0.0000 \leq \alpha \Rightarrow$ Reject H_o (Acceptable risk of making a type I error)
Step 6: There is enough evidence, at the 10% significance level, to show that there is a difference between the proportion of text message users among the younger and older age groups.

b) There were at least 5 people using and not using text messaging services in each sample, so the requirements have been met.

c) We need the z-scores for 90% confidence.

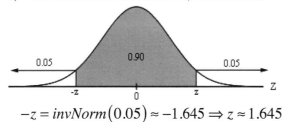

$$-z = invNorm(0.05) \approx -1.645 \Rightarrow z \approx 1.645$$

$$(0.6887 - 0.3516) \pm 1.645 \cdot \sqrt{\frac{0.6887 * 0.3113}{212} + \frac{0.3516 * 0.6484}{219}}$$

$$= 0.3371 \pm 0.0745 \Rightarrow p_1 - p_2 \in (0.2626, \ 0.4116)$$

d) We are 90% confident that the proportion of people in the 18 – 39 age group that use text messaging is somewhere between 26.26% and 41.16% higher than for the 40 – 54 age group.

e) If $p_1 - p_2 \in (0.2626, 0.4116)$
$\Rightarrow p_1 - p_2 > 0 \Rightarrow p_1 > p_2 \Rightarrow H_o : p_1 = p_2$
is false $\Rightarrow$ Reject H_o.

f) I would recommend that the focus their marking dollars on the younger group. A much higher percentage of this group is interested in what they are selling than in the older group.

12) a) Step 1: We are trying to show that the second attempt is "better", meaning a higher percentage, than the first attempt,

so we get:
$$H_o : \mu_1 \geq \mu_2$$
$$H_a : \mu_1 < \mu_2$$

Step 2: $\alpha = 0.05$

Step 3: Since $\overline{d}$ is not given, we will find it using the calculator. Enter the before values into L1 and the after values into L2. Then let L3 = L2 – L1. Finally choose STAT > CALC > 1-Var Stats L3 and we get:

$$\overline{d} \approx -2.3333, \ s_d \approx 2.2254, \ n = 15$$

$$t = \frac{\overline{d}}{s_d / \sqrt{n}} = \frac{-2.3333}{2.2254 / \sqrt{15}} \approx -4.061$$

Step 4: $H_a : \mu_1 < \mu_2 \Rightarrow$ This is a left-tailed test. $df = n - 1 = 14$

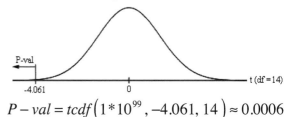

$$P - val = tcdf(1 * 10^{99}, -4.061, 14) \approx 0.0006$$

Step 5: $P - val \approx 0.0006 \leq \alpha \Rightarrow$ Reject H_o (Acceptable risk of making a type I error)

Step 6: There is enough evidence, at the 5% significance level, to show that the second attempt at a song will be, on average, better than the first attempt.

b) We need the t-scores for 90% confidence.

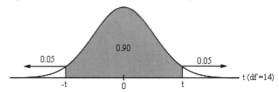

From the t-table, we get $t_{0.05} = 1.761$.

$$-2.33 \pm 1.761 \cdot \frac{2.2254}{\sqrt{15}} = -2.33 \pm 1.01$$

$$\Rightarrow \mu_1 - \mu_2 \in (-3.34, \ -1.32)$$

c) We are 90% confident that the average percentage of notes successfully played is somewhere between 1.32% and 3.34% higher on the second attempt of a song.

d) If $\mu_1 - \mu_2 \in (-3.34, -1.32)$
$\Rightarrow \mu_1 - \mu_2 < 0 \Rightarrow \mu_1 < \mu_2$
$\Rightarrow H_o : \mu_1 \geq \mu_2$ is false $\Rightarrow$ Reject H_o

e) Since $15 \leq n = 15 < 30$, we must hope that the before and after differences in the population are not severely skewed.

f) Since we rejected H_o, it is not a type II error, it is either a type I error (if H_o is true), or a correct decision (if H_o is false). We perceive the risk of a type I error to only be about 0.06%.